creative techniques
FOR RUG HOOKERS

By Donna Hrkman

Library of Congress Cataloging-in-Publication Data

Hrkman, Donna, author.
Creative techniques for rug hookers / Donna Hrkman.—First edition.
    pages cm
ISBN 978-0-8117-1334-4
1. Rugs, Hooked. I. Title.
TT850.H745 2015
746.7'4—dc23
                                        2015028943

CONTENTS

Detail of **Koi** (See the full rug on page 90.)

Rug hooking is more than a hobby for me. It's a means of self-expression; it's how I communicate and how I see the world. I have learned so much about myself and my art through rug hooking that I want to share what I've learned over the past ten years as a rug hooker.

Rug hooking is art. I have been an artist all my life and have come to embrace the art of rug hooking as my greatest means of creative expression. Rug hooking includes all of the aspects of art I need: design, composition, color, texture, line, depth . . . Whatever I need to create, I can do it with wool.

I have a long history of exploring artistic expression, starting with my fine arts education and experience as a painter and sculptor. I have worked in figural drawing, technical drawing, and portraits. I have used charcoal, colored pencil, and pen and ink. I've painted in oils, acrylics, watercolors, and temperas. I've quilled, cross-stitched, quilted, and stenciled. I have done freelance illustrations for craft catalogs and designed clothing and home decor fabric for a major fabric company.

These experiences have given me the background and experience to be a rug hooker. I have learned how to interpret artistic elements and

apply them to the constraints of linen and wool. I push myself with every new rug to create something different and wonderful. That's what I want to share with others.

To be creative you must open your mind. Sometimes it means taking a baby step into the next level of imagination; sometimes it means taking a large leap of faith. What I want to do is open the door a little wider and show you some of the techniques I use in my rug hooking. You may already know some of these techniques. What I hope to do is challenge you to see things with fresh eyes, whether it's looking at your subject matter differently or evaluating the techniques you already use and taking them further. I want *you* to open the door to *your* creativity just a little bit wider to see what's there.

I'm offering suggestions and directions on how to get your foot through that door. I explain some of the techniques I use, like creating depth through shading, hooking realistic portraits, creating wallpaper backgrounds, and more.

Come on in. Look around. See what you think about these techniques and get ready to push the door open wide to your own creativity. I've got some keys right here . . .

C'mon! Let's get busy!

It's hookin' time!

CHAPTER 1

Elements of Design

Detail of **Blue Mermaiden** (See the full rug on page 96.)

When you approach a rug hooking project, what do you do? There are a few things to keep in mind about creating a rug, and it's a good idea to lay out your design in advance. If you have the basic structure planned out, it will be easier to make changes if you need to. Think of it as a master floor plan. You know where all of the rooms are, and if you need to make adjustments, you'll have an overview and foundation to work from.

I don't hook commercial patterns, and so I am not going to address how to do that. Those of you who do hook commercial patterns already have the basic structure in a pattern on which to build your rug, and your primary concern will be color choice. But if you're interested in creating your own rug design, I have some tips to share.

FIND A REFERENCE

Have a source. It could be a photo, an illustration, or a painting; get permission if you need it or be more creative and draw it yourself. Have something as a reference so you can stay consistent in your hooking. Do your research.

START ON PAPER

If you are starting from scratch, you can draw your design out freehand on a small piece of paper if you like and then take it to your local print shop to enlarge it to the size you want to hook. Or take your source and use one of the techniques I use to enlarge it my designs: the grid process, tracing it from your source using red dot or blue grid interfacing, or by drawing through a screen to transfer the design.

Your goal is to draw up a design, either from a photo or drawing, and make it the size you want to hook without distorting it in the process. Drawing on tracing paper is my choice because it lets me trace elements when I need to, and it also lets me fold over the paper for repeats or for centering parts of the design. Tracing paper is available in large pads, too, so you have plenty of room to draw your pattern.

If you're working from a photo, lay a 1″ grid (drawn out on a clear acetate sheet) over it, then draw out a larger grid on your tracing paper. If you want the design twice as large as the photo, draw 2″ squares; three times as large would require 3″ squares. The grid allows you to transfer the design square by square and match the lines from your source, so there's less chance of distortion or disruption.

FOCUS ON COLOR

A lot of elements go into a successful design. Color is only one of them. Look at rugs you like and make notes on why you like them. Is it the color scheme? Is it the balance? The scale? The composition? Figuring out what you like will help you achieve it in your own work.

Colors have a huge impact in rug hooking because, like in paintings, color is the expression of the feeling in the rug. Bright, cheerful color can be a joyful dance for the eyes, whereas dark, somber

color provides a restful, calming effect. Contrasting colors make a rug more lively and active visually; more monochromatic tones will be softer and more muted.

Here are some of my color tips:

- **Avoid black for shading.** Black can create a visual hole in your rug, and nobody wants a hole—of any kind!—in a rug. Shade with darker complementary colors; for example, use a dark olive green on a red surface. You can use black when the subject dictates it, like for the pupil of the eye. But otherwise, if your reference material shows black in the subject, use a very dark blue or brown for less harsh contrast. If you are hooking a black dog, for example, use a variety of blues, greens, and grays for shading and definition.

- **Pinpoint the light.** Define a light source and location for that source in your design and stick with it throughout the composition. Traditionally, in classic painting, light sources come from the upper right-hand corner. You don't have to follow that rule, but wherever your light is, stay consistent. The highlights that define shape in objects have to match across the plane of the design. In highlighting eyes, for example, the bright spots have to match in each eye, or you will get "googly" eyes, and that's not good.

- **Use shading for three dimensions.** Wherever possible, when choosing colors for a three-dimensional subject, like a house or a tree, choose several shades of the same color to show depth. Remember: light, medium, and dark. If you have a Red Delicious apple, for example, select several shades of red as well as some yellow and green for highlights and shading. The play of light determines shading, and shading determines dimension. Flat color will produce flat objects.
- **Become a squinter.** Squinting helps your perception by blurring the detail and allows you to see the bulk of your design. By blurring the detail, you can "read" the composition more easily and catch any potential color imbalances in your work.
- **Stay alert for uneven balance.** Rug elements can sometimes become too busy or visually heavy. Hold your rug up to a mirror to detect uneven balance. This technique is especially helpful to check for proportion when you are hooking faces. You can also simply flip the rug over and look at it from the back. When you look at a rug from the back, you will get clearer definition of your hooked lines. From the front, the loops expand and blend, but those loops are condensed and more precise on the back and therefore easier to see.
- **Establish good contrast.** Good contrast needs to happen in two places: in your design and in your color plan. Use complementary colors for shading and for definition. Create sharp edges and definition with bits of darker line when you need to make something stand out. A recognizable dark-versus-light ratio will make your rug more interesting. Be sure to have brights and darks in your piece for even more interest.
- **Choose colors based on style.** The type of rug you choose to hook will determine your color palette. Primitive rugs have darker, duller color palettes because they are, by definition, meant to look older and more worn. The primitive style also uses wider cuts of wool, so there is less room for shading and highlighting.
- **Think of color as your own playground.** You can hook with any range of color you like. Brights, darks, textures, solids . . . The wool is yours to manipulate and combine for countless combinations. If you're not sure what colors will work best together, do a layout with colored pencils— and don't forget to throw in a couple contrasting colors for balance. A color wheel is invaluable when you want to pick complementary colors, shades, and tints.

UNDERSTAND THE EFFECTS OF LINE

Line is another important element in rug hooking. Fine lines—fine cut strips of wool—equal greater detail; wide lines—wide cut strips—equal less detail. That's not to say that some level of detail can't be achieved in a primitive-style rug, it's just that shading and definition are easier when you use thinner strips.

The use of line in your rugs will make a big difference in the overall appearance of your rug. I make it a practice to never just "fill in" areas of my rugs. Everything has direction. If I am hooking animals, my lines will reflect the direction of their fur or feathers. If I am hooking humans, then the lines will indicate how the skin is shaped to cover the muscle and skeletal structure. If I am hooking a landscape, the lines will define the shape of hills, grass, trees, or clouds. Seldom is anything perfectly straight in my rugs because seldom is anything perfectly straight in nature.

USE TEXTURE IN BACKGROUNDS

I always hook a background with "texture," and I don't mean tweed. What I strive for in backgrounds is a complement to the items in the foreground, because the foreground motifs are the ones I want to show off. The background doesn't need to be a flat solid color because very seldom in our lives are we posed against a flat, solid background. Even a wall needs some small degree of texture. Using curly lines instead of straight ones is a smart way to go, because repeated straight lines in a rug can lead to a splitting of the rug between those lines. It's naturally going to fold on the lines and create unwanted breaks in the design.

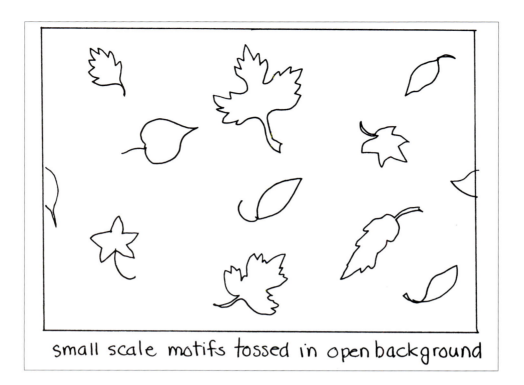

small scale motifs tossed in open background

large scale motifs tossed in open background

PAY ATTENTION TO SCALE

Scale is important—don't discount scale. I have seen some nice rugs that could have been 10 times better if the rug hooker had enlarged certain elements and eliminated more background. A design that is made up of a "toss" (a flat background filled with separate elements like leaves or flowers) needs to connect those elements in some way, even if they aren't touching.

Some patterns have elements so small that they look lost in the vast area around them. To make elements stand out, make them larger and even bump them into each other here and there.

Scale also adds dimension. If you have a dog and a little boy in your composition, don't make the dog's features larger proportionally than the little boy's. Keep scale in mind: sure, some dogs' heads are bigger than a human's head, but make sure the proportions are right.

representational scale

non-representational scale

GET THE PERSPECTIVE RIGHT

Perspective is another key design element. If you have a house in the background, keep the surrounding elements in perspective. Don't hook a big house and tree and then add a ridiculously large bird and dog in that same plane. If that bird on the roof can't fit through the front door, then there's something wrong! The exception, of course, is a primitive rug design where elements are drawn deliberately out of proportion to convey a sense of naiveté.

Remember: Elements closer to you are larger; elements farther from you are smaller. Closer elements have more detail and color than smaller, farther-away elements. Close equals sharper, brighter, clearer. Far equals duller, dimmer, softer.

Don't sharpen images that are supposed to appear distant, because your eye will bring them forward, which ruins the feeling of depth you're trying to achieve.

Creating a rug of your own design can be a challenge, but the rewards are well worth the extra work. The satisfaction and pride you feel will motivate you to create more of your own designs. You are the artist, and your rug reflects your creativity and talent and yours alone. Rug hooking is a fabulous art form, because we rug hookers get the pleasure of playing with color and all the other elements that painters do, plus we get the extra bonus of texture: art you can touch! Don't be afraid to create!

CHAPTER 2

Create Depth and Dimension

Grand Canyon, 28" x 44", #4- & 6-cut wool on linen, 2008.

Rugs have limitless potential as works of art. Just like paintings, a hooked rug can be flat and two-dimensional, or it can be so realistic that one wants to touch it to see if it's really a flat surface.

Realistic rugs are representational of a three-dimensional subject, so creating depth and a believable look are important. Knowing how it's done is not as difficult as one might imagine.

Artistic design elements apply to any creative endeavor, whether it's a drawing, a painting, or a rug. These basic elements are the foundation for making something look like it could come right off the paper, canvas, or linen.

EXCEPTIONS TO THE RULE

■ Primitive rugs are known for their simplicity, flatness, exaggeration of scale, dull colors, and basic shapes in design. They are not detailed or shaded to any great degree, and they convey a certain naive quality that is charming and historical. Primitives are highly stylized, which is to say that they are not representational in the subject matter they depict. So the use of shading and dimension are not of key importance in this style of rug.

CONSIDER THESE DESIGN ELEMENTS
AS YOU PLAN YOUR NEXT RUG

- **A focal point:** an area within the design where the eye goes first

- **Overlapping visual planes:** layers of depth that lie over one another from front to back or top to bottom

- **Prominent planes:** bright and sharply defined planes that stand out

- **Receding planes:** duller and less defined planes that recede

- **Shading:** objects that are shaded to create a three-dimensional look

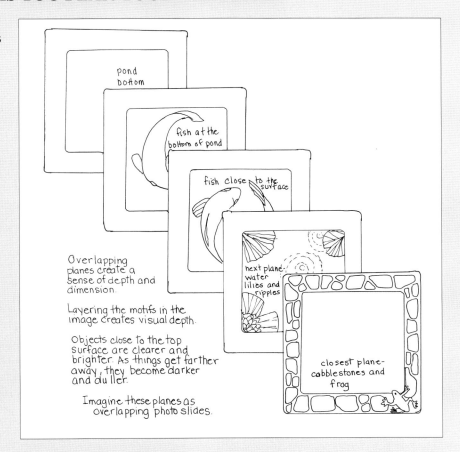

Overlapping planes create a sense of depth and dimension.

Layering the motifs in the image creates visual depth.

Objects close to the top surface are clearer and brighter. As things get farther away, they become darker and duller.

Imagine these planes as overlapping photo slides.

- Oriental rugs are also rather two-dimensional by design. They are rich in pattern and color, feature vividly created images, and are very stylized. They generally follow traditional patterns with fine detail, and a degree of shading is found in those with floral or animal motifs, but the sense of depth is not as important as the portrayal of elements in the design.

Realistic rugs are representational of a three-dimensional subject, so creating depth and a believable look are important. Knowing how it's done is not as difficult as one might imagine.

CREATE DEPTH AND DIMENSION

Koi (See a larger view on page 90.)

I am a Pisces, so I am drawn to designs that feature water and fish. I decided to create a rug that would feature a koi pond, and I wanted to capture the wonderful, multi-layered look of a small, controlled environment. My goal was to recreate the visual image of the many planes of color, definition, and depth that make a koi pond so beautiful.

The layout for the pond began with a clear representation of the fish. I studied several sources and decided to use two common breeds of koi: a vivid yellow-orange with bright orange accents and a bright coral red with patches of black and white. I knew these colors would enhance the design and make the fish stand out clearly in the rug.

The surface of the pond, my first plane, had to be clear. I used a couple of methods to make that first plane clear. First, I added lily pads and water lilies to define the first level. They rest on the surface. Second, I further defined the surface of the water with a few circular ripples in lighter tones to introduce movement in the water. The lily pads overlap one another and fill the area in the corners of the pond design. They are important, but they are not the focal point. The fish are the focal point, as they circle around each other, mimicking Pisces, one ending where the other begins. This visual movement fits nicely within the square area of the pond and keeps the design from becoming stagnant. The fish are the largest and brightest elements in the rug and the only elements in motion. Viewers see the fish first; then, everything else follows.

The water below the two koi forms a second plane. I hooked it in darker colors, using swirled lines to indicate the depth of the pond and provide a foil for the brightness of the fish. If you look closely, you can just barely see a shadowy image of another fish, swimming beneath the yellow koi. He's the scavenger fish, the one you see at the bottom of every pond, slowly circling the bottom for scraps falling from above. This fish helps to define that lowest plane in the rug, giving the other levels a range of depth.

The outer border, the cobbled path, is also a plane. It becomes a frame for the pond and defines the nearest plane for the viewer. A small frog sits in the corner of the cobblestones, and he is the highest image on the rug. He leads the eye to the central image of the fish, but he does not stand out as clearly as the fish do. He provides another element of layering that makes the rug seem to be dimensional.

These layered planes make a design image that does more than sit flatly across the surface. By layering planes, using variations in color and value, you can create your own dimensional surfaces.

These layered planes make a design image that does more than sit flatly across the surface. By layering planes, using variations in color and value, you can create your own dimensional surfaces.

Detail of **Koi**
(See the full rug
on page 90.)

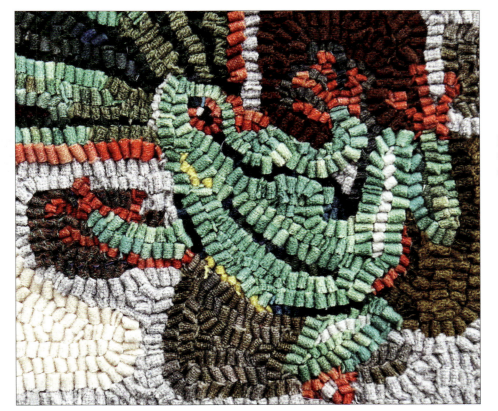

Detail of **Koi**
(See the full rug
on page 90.)

DEPTH AND DIMENSION IN A LANDSCAPE

Detail of **Grand Canyon** (See the full rug on page 6.)

Remember: Brighter, more defined images advance or come forward in the design, while duller, darker images recede. Elements in the design that are meant to be focal points should be more detailed and shaded to create the feeling of a three-dimensional object, with highlights and shadows in the appropriate places.

In *Grand Canyon*, the depth is essential to convey the vast expanse of the landscape. Where can one find a more dramatic range of color, texture, and sheer beauty? In order to represent the remarkable depth and width of the canyon, I had to find a good source photo and draw it to capture that amazing feeling.

I found a photo taken by a nature photographer and asked his permission to use it. He was more than happy to share it with me, and once the rug was completed, I sent him a color photo of the finished piece. He was excited to see his work interpreted in another form.

The photo was of a wide expanse of the canyon, and I wanted to incorporate the darker depths as well as the sheer drop of the cliffs. The clouds in the distance were as lovely and as integral to the

design as the canyon itself. So this landscape presented itself as a challenge to capture all those different dimensions and planes, from the faraway background to the sharply outlined shrubbery in the front of the photo.

I used a grid technique to transfer the design from the photo to the linen backing. Once the grid was in place, I had a good idea of the layout and what elements I would need to shade for depth and what areas would need to be lighter. I broke the design plan into three main areas: the background, the middle ground, and the foreground.

Elements in the background are the least detailed. While they are still catching light, the lines are soft and the shading is blurry. One can still recognize the cliffs and clouds, but they do not contain the amount of fine detail and shading as those in the nearer portions of the rug.

The middle ground is deeper and darker as it encompasses the floor and walls of the canyon. Deep, rich reds with veins of lighter shades run diagonally through the image, leading the eye back into the mountains and cliffs. The middle ground is more richly colored and shaded than the background, and it comes forward ahead of the distant

Grid layout of **Grand Canyon**

Grid with **Grand Canyon** well underway.

cliffs by virtue of the deeper shades and colors.

The foreground is the clearest, brightest, and most detailed area. It is the frontal plane of the landscape. Here we find a stony, graveled outcropping of rock with a scraggly bush atop it. From this vantage point we see the entire expanse of the landscape. By hooking the foreground lighter and with more detail, the viewer can see beyond what is directly in front of her and over the edge, into the deep reaches of this wonderful place.

The depth, the breakdown into three planes, and the use of light and dark contrast work together to make a believable landscape.

CREATING DIMENSION IN HOOKED ANIMALS

USE TEXTURE

When hooking animals, the easiest way to convey a three-dimensional look is through detail in texture and shading. If you are hooking a furry animal, like a dog, cat, or llama, keep in mind that the texture of the fur or fleece makes all the difference in the world in creating dimension. It's important to keep in mind that how you portray the animal's fur will determine if that animal becomes believable and real.

Birds have their own variety of textures. Feathers can lie flat and smooth or they can be ruffled and fluffed like a turkey. How the feathers lie and their direction creates patterns and textures that we can duplicate in our rugs. From the tiniest detailed wing of a hummingbird to the glorious plumes of an ostrich, the way we hook the lines and textures will make our creatures come alive.

Detail of **Barred Owl** (See the full rug on page 104.)

How feathers lie and their direction creates patterns and textures that we can duplicate in our rugs. The way we hook the lines and textures will make our creations come alive.

DON'T SKIMP ON SHADING

We shade subjects to make them believable.

- Heads look rounded if they are highlighted from one side and shaded on the other.

- Shading follows contours; it's not just a gray line around an element.

- Shading can use many colors that blend into the shape of the subject.

- Reflected light isn't just a white highlight; it can also be a brighter tint of the colors of the subject.

Curly, the Llama, 20" x 26", #4- and 6-cut wool on linen. Designed and hooked by Donna Hrkman, Dayton, Ohio, 2006.

USE LINE DIRECTION

In *Curly the Llama,* the direction of lines becomes important in creating a believable animal face. Llama and alpaca fleece textures vary, so showing the degree of texture helps define each animal. Curly has, as his name implies, a thick, curly coat of coarse fleece. Directional lines define the direction his hair grows. You can see the slope of his nose, the area of his cheekbones, the shape of his eyes, and the outline of his mouth all by virtue of the lightness and darkness and direction of the hooked lines.

As the area of the llama's fleece expands, shading and direction of line are important. His fleece hangs in thick cords, so there is a lot of layering of color and value. Darker areas of fleece are behind and beneath the lighter cords, which are highlighted and stand out against the shadowed areas. Wavy lines suggest curly cords of fleece as they hang down. Lighter shades across his neck contrast against the darker shades beneath his chin and jawline. These areas of varied highlights and shadows make him look real—and realistically textured.

IT ALL COMES BACK TO TEXTURE

- With dogs, coats run the gamut from flat, sleek fur of a beagle to long, flowing locks of an afghan hound to the curly hair of a poodle. Cat fur can be short and sleek or fluffy and luxurious. Then there are sheep and foxes and otters . . . Whatever your source photos shows you, try to create that texture. Pay attention to the flow of the fur or hair or fleece as you hook each area. Directional hooking is important here.

Directional lines help create the texture of the fleece and shape of the head.

Dogs in Water,
30" x 24", #3- and
4-cut wool on linen.
Designed and hooked
by Donna Hrkman,
Dayton, Ohio, 2011.

USE SHADING

Shading becomes a key element in several different ways in *Dogs in Water*. The white dogs aren't actually white. They are a combination of many shades, including cream, beige, tan, gray, blue, green, and yellow. They stand in water and their fur is dripping and hanging in strands, not fluffy and dry. Notice the variations in how their colors reflect in the surface of the water and how the water is reflected in the colors of their fur. Keep in mind that the colors and textures allow these dogs to look as if they could step right out of the water to be petted.

Shadows indicate depth in portraiture, making it seem as if the subject is ready to step out of the frame. When you hear the word "shadow," you are likely to think of a silhouette cast on the ground on a sunny day, or maybe the long shadows of trees cast by the setting sun. We see these every day of our lives and don't think twice about them.

Shading and shadows are important in rendering realistic subjects because they define objects and solidify them in a given space. Shading indicates texture, shape, dimension, and surface. A shadow beneath an object gives it a foundation and grounds it in the environment.

Shading defines the shape and dimension by showing where the object exists in space. In this rug, dark shading in the lower parts of the dogs indicate that one dog is standing closer to the viewer than the other. The shading beneath them indicates that they are standing knee-deep in water. Their ears create shadows on the fur of their necks, and the wavy lines of shadow show how their fur grows and hangs from their bodies.

The contrast of dark versus light, no matter how subtle, makes the difference in distinguishing different areas of the rug and makes the main subjects stand out. By using a consistent location for the light source, you can shade areas for believable dimension and depth.

SURROUNDINGS AND BACKGROUND ARE IMPORTANT

If you are hooking an animal in its natural habitat, hook in a believable background. A polar bear in a tropical setting won't make sense. It pays to do some research when hooking wild animals to make sure they're in the right environment.

Do not let elements of the background become too detailed or bright, because they will come forward in the rug. The elements of the background should give your creatures a sense of place.

USE CONTRAST TO CREATE DIMENSION

Native American Boy (See a larger view on page 91.)

Using contrast is another way to create depth and dimension. Color becomes a nonissue in a monochromatic rug, like Native American Boy. What defines the shape and dimension of a subject in any rug, colorful or monochromatic, is the amount of detail and degrees of contrast in the composition. Elements of design, like clear lines and a great difference in the degree of dark to light, will enable the artist to make an image look real and solid.

I hooked *Native American Boy* in a deep purple/brown color that encompasses nine levels of shading from the darkest value to the lightest in white. This range provides a degree of shading possibilities that let the image become believable and real.

It was important to me that the boy have a strong presence. His deep, penetrating gaze was what drew me to this image initially, and it was important that I capture that depth. If the eyes are truly the window to the soul, then this child had a deep and serious soul. So my challenge was to use the range of values from dark to light and combine them in a believable, realistic composition that would bring the beauty and spirit of the boy and show the depth and dimension of his appearance. He was captured in his own place and time, and I wanted to be respectful of that.

I always start with the eyes in my portrait work, and with this child, it was a serious task to capture those eyes. If they did not convey his expression from the photograph, then the whole spirit of the rug would be lost. So I drew them carefully and made certain that they were perfect. I hooked the pupils and eyelids, and then hooked the iris using several shades of the brown to make it look dimensional. I added the highlights—that burst of life that indicates moisture in the eye, and makes it look real—last. Once the eyes were properly in place, I moved around the eye sockets to the nose and mouth, and then I filled in the rest of the face according to the shading and highlights of the photo.

One of greatest areas of contrast in this rug is in the blanket wrapped around his shoulders. In order to create a blanket that looked real, I studied how the folds of the blanket fell and where they overlapped. The deepest contrasts are between the shadowed folds and the more exposed areas where the blanket is the whitest and most brightly lit.

By using techniques that create distance, depth, detail, and dimension, you can create a realistic piece of art that is deep, believable, and visually textured.

Detail of **Native American Boy**

The lines of hooking had to match the contours of the wool blanket as it wrapped around his shoulders. The bands of dark stripes in the wool blanket had to match up and make sense as they were gathered and folded. By creating strong areas of dark versus light, I made a striped blanket that looks like actual wool.

These techniques will work for you too when you create a rug that cries out for a feeling of depth and dimension. It doesn't take much to turn a flat, two-dimensional rug design into a rug that has that richness. Keep in mind that the focus of your rug out can be enhanced by using color, shading, texture, and line.

By using techniques that create distance, depth, detail, and dimension, you can create a realistic piece of art that is a deep, believable, and visually textured. It's fun to make something so successful that you know someone will have to touch it to be sure it's really a rug!

CHAPTER 3

Add Texture and Embellishment

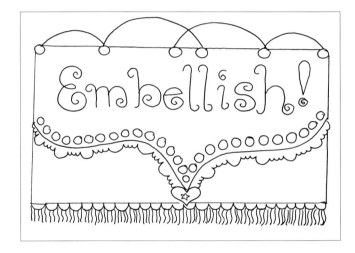

Wool is the paint for rug hooking canvases. With our hooks as the brush, we fill the blank spaces with lovely, colored strips and create a beautiful surface. We use solids, spot-dyes, dip-dyes, and myriad textures to create the wonderful visual experience of our rugs.

The possibilities are endless. By using all solid wool, all textures, or mixing a variety of wools, we create rich and visually interesting rugs just by using strips of wool—and that's how most of us work.

Sometimes it's fun to play with other paints in the paint box. By using other types of fabrics and embellishments, rug hookers can add a more dimensional look to their work. And it can be as bold or as subtle as necessary to get the desired look.

What can be added? In my work I've incorporated yarns and ribbons, pieces of jewelry, metal gears, pronged metal brads, and countless other interesting bits to make my rugs more interesting and to highlight certain elements in the design. You can add wool roving, embroidery threads, beads, and other fabrics like denim, paisley, silk, or cotton. Each new texture will act differently as it's incorporated into the rug, so practicing with the materials in a sample piece of foundation is a good idea.

One of the primary things to keep in mind when adding embellishments is how they will be attached. There is no single method to attach them,

but you should keep one very important factor in mind: embellishments should not harm or weaken the rug or the foundation.

When adding embellishments to rugs, make sure that they are safely secured. Be sure to leave a degree of play between the items you attach and the backing/hooked loops so the embellishment doesn't compress the hooking too much yet stays secure without flopping around. If you attach metal pieces, make sure that they don't sever the thread that holds them in place and confirm that the knots and stitching in the linen are secure.

Experiment on a small sample of hooking to see how the extra pieces will lie or fit into the area you want to decorate; then, you can make adjustments in the attachment as you proceed on your larger piece.

YARN AS EMBELLISHMENT

Some rugs are hooked entirely with yarn, so it's no big deal to incorporate yarn into a rug made with wool strips. Yarn hooks easily enough, and it's a natural texture. I find the greatest difference is how "steerable" wool strips are versus how wool yarn feels as it's pulled through the linen. Because wool strips are thinner and flatter, they can be pulled up next to each other and form smooth lines that create a uniform surface. Yarn is round, so even if you are pulling uniform loops, the loops don't lie flat next to each other. Yarn loops expand to fill the areas differently than wool strips and don't follow a direction.

You can use your hook to pull loops of yarn or wool thread or other long textured pieces through the backing. Sometimes, if the added texture is thin, you can hook the wool strips first and then add the thinner pieces of yarn or thread over the loops. Or you can hold the thread or yarn together with the wool strips as a unit and hook them together. Ribbon can be added the same way. Because ribbon is both thin and flat, you can determine how it lies in your design. It can twist and become a very thin texture, or it can be pulled flat and become a wider texture. Experiment with these materials and decide which look you like best.

Detail of **LLarry, the Llama** (See the full rug on page 25.)

While I was hooking a llama portrait, I attended a livestock breed show for llamas and alpacas and purchased several skeins of alpaca yarn in natural colors. As I hooked the llama's neck and head, I decided to add the long pieces of yarn to represent the loose strands of fleece.

I measured strands of the yarn for his forelock and some for the top of his head that would fall down alongside his neck. The goal was to create a believable looking mane for Llarry while keeping it loose and free. I knotted the ends of the yarn at one end and pulled the strands through the hooked loops to lie across the surface. I could have stitched them in a certain layout for his bangs, but I decided not to; I preferred that they be loose. Llarry has a whimsical attitude about him, and I thought the free-flowing bangs would suit that look.

WOOL AS EMBELLISHMENT

Cat Tongue,
15" x 17", #8-cut
wool on linen.
Designed and
hooked by
Donna Hrkman,
Dayton, Ohio,
2003.

Early on in my rug hooking, I hooked in wider cuts and created more primitive-style pieces. I often hooked mats that featured stylized cats. One of my favorite design devices was to hook little pink tongues on the cats' mouths. It was fun, cute, and gave a bit of charm to the cats—and it's about as easy as anything. I just cut a strip of cat tongue–pink wool to about $1/2''$ in length, rounded the corners of one end, and then pulled the strip through the hooked loops of the cat's mouth with the rounded end exposed. I trimmed the tail close to the loops to hide it. It's a simple thing, and it makes adorable cat faces!

A THOUGHT ABOUT WHISKERS

- Don't worry about hooking whiskers into your animal portrait. Unless you hook a very large animal head, the whiskers will be a very tiny size—and even fine hooking will be too thick. You can just ignore them, or you can use a couple of other methods to put them in.

- One way to simulate whiskers is to attach fishing line, knot it at the end, pull it through, and then tuck in at the ends. Or use embroidery floss or wool floss. One creative hooker uses bits of horse tail hair. It's coarse and sturdy and lies pretty flat. Experiment with the material of your choice, but don't sweat the hooking!

USING TEXTURED WOOL FOR ANIMALS

Textured wool strips can also be used to create a believable texture for an animal. Bird feathers should look feathery, sheeps' fleece should look woolly, and dog fur should look furry. Some textured wools will hook up quickly and easily; others need extra care but will give you amazing results.

Owl Eye (See sidebar on page 58.)

Sometimes a simple piece of heavily textured wool can work miracles. The key is to mix several types of textures to achieve believable results. For example, in *Owl Eye*, a sample I use in classes, I hooked different types and textures of wool all in one small hooked piece. They work together to make a realistic-looking portion of an owl's face.

I hooked the eye of the owl with solid wool strips. Solid wool is good for hooking eyes because it creates a smooth surface. Adding a white high-light makes the eye look wet, and therefore alive. Smooth and shiny eyes look real. The beak is also smooth, a shaded variety of grays, browns, and golds.

The other wools are all varieties of textures. The rust-colored wool along the cheek and side of the owl's face is a dyed houndstooth, which gives a lesser degree of texture, but just enough to indicate feathering along the owl's face. The heavier textures come into play around the beak, the brow, and the top of his head.

I looked carefully at the source photo and selected wool textures that approximate the living texture of the owl's feathers. The heavier the texture of the wool, the more it looks like the textures of the feathers. The key to using these heavier, looser textured wools is to be gentle. Some of the wool is so loosely woven that it cannot be cut fine. For those wools, just cut wide or use scissors. Hooking these loose weaves into the rug takes a little more time and finesse to keep them from shredding to strings, but the final result will be worth it.

Combining solids, medium textures, and heavily textured wools will make an interesting and dramatic piece. Why not play around with some of that wool you might never have considered before because you thought that it was too loose or too frayed? Experiment and play with textures—you'll like it!

FABRIC AND TEXTILE EMBELLISHMENTS

Detail of **Alzheimer's Rug** (See the full rug on page 92.)

You can use textures from special fabrics and embellishments in your compositions simply as a design element, to enhance a certain portion of the rug, to focus on a specific area, or to add a fun texture. Sometimes, however, the embellishments' contribution to the design becomes greater than that.

When I hooked my *Alzheimer's Rug,* I wanted to show that the woman with the disease was coming apart. The concept of her losing all of her best and brightest parts, her memory, her abilities, her sense of self—all of that became literal for me as a designer. I drew the pattern with her graying hair blowing out behind her. Her hair included hooked words that represented her lost brightness among the bits of gray wool and colored silk ribbon.

These small but visceral elements are key to showing her literal coming apart. The rough textures of the yarns imply the fraying of her psyche and the unraveling of her mind. The colored bits of silk ribbon are more delicate. They represent those fragile, emotional bits that are being pulled away from her by the disease. I used just a few embellishments in this rug, and they aren't large, but they all have a significance.

SPECIAL EMBELLISHMENTS

Detail of **Steampunk Reverie** (See the full rug on page 101.)

I fell in love with Steampunk years ago and often thought about creating a rug with a Steampunk theme. Steampunk is an active art movement that celebrates a style of motion, history, and ingenuity. I love the creative aspect of how people create art in this style. It encompasses the look of Victorian England and the development of the Industrial Age, represented in fashion, architecture, jewelry, and more. Steampunk includes elements like steam engines, dirigibles, corsets, clocks, top hats, gears, ravens, owls, Gatling guns, and just about any other funky combination of mechanical wizardry and bustles you can think of. In other words, it's fun and creative.

Steampunk Reverie is loaded with embellishments. The purpose of creating this piece was to highlight the addition of bits and pieces of goodies to create dimension and texture, which is a key element of Steampunk work. I collected pieces of

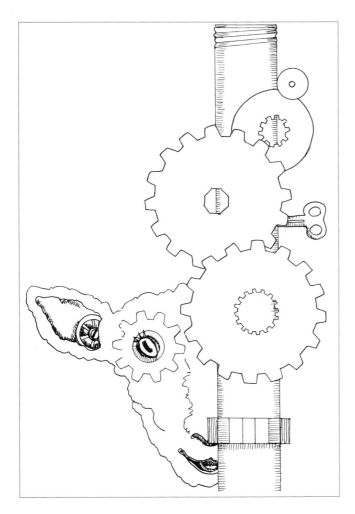

Ribbon

Jewelry

jewelry in the Victorian style and found metal gears, handles, brads, nails, and screws to use. The scrapbooking aisles in craft stores are filled with wonderful doodads and pieces of treasure that can add so much to a period piece like mine.

The most difficult part of making this rug was waiting until it was finished to start adding the embellishments. As I hooked each new area, my mind was racing toward the finish when I would finally be able to add the pieces of metal and jewelry to the rug, creating the image I had in my head from Day One of the process. It didn't take long to finish the rug, and then I looked at the embellishments with a sense of anticipation and excitement.

There are a lot of different pieces added to the Steampunk Rug. I hooked all the elements first, like the gears in her hair and hat and behind her in the background. These are all part of the composition, and even if they would be covered by actual pieces of metal or jewelry at the end, they still needed to be there. The exception to this is the ribbon that frames her dress bodice. It's a piece of navy blue grosgrain ribbon that I ruched (gathered) with a long running stitch down the

center of the ribbon. I left the area for that ribbon unhooked so the ribbon would fit in the trench and not stick up too far on the dress. I stitched the ribbon by hand through the linen backing with navy blue quilt thread.

Some elements needed more than just stitching. The bird's nest brooch is stitched and wired into the brim of her hat to keep it secure. Other pieces were much easier to attach. The metal brads with screw heads could be attached by gently nudging them between loops and spreading the brad arms apart on the back. Some of the small brads are secured through gears, so both elements are attached with the brad. The little pipe handles are attached through the linen backing at four spots on the pipe background.

These embellishments were key in creating a Steampunk rug that celebrates the blending of rich fabrics and funky metal mechanical parts. The rug would have conveyed it without the embellishments, but not to the degree that it does with them.

There are so many avenues to take when it comes to adding extra textures to your work. More and more rug hookers are using different textures and means of decoration to create wonderful, artistic rugs. Don't feel limited to just wool strips to create your piece. The key is making the embellishments look like an integral part of the design, not just something tacked on at random.

So go ahead and try some beads, bangles, baubles, and braids. They might just be the dazzle you want!

CHAPTER 4

Special Border Designs

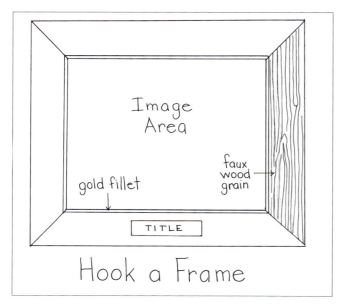

Image Area

gold fillet

faux wood grain

TITLE

Hook a Frame

treatments, while others need the border as a significant part of the design.

Borders are a great way to add interest to a rug. They serve many purposes, including enhancing the main body of the rug, either by providing contrast or reinforcing color, motifs, or pattern. They serve as a frame, much like a mat and frame around a photograph. Borders anchor the visual edge of the rug so the viewer's eye doesn't just abruptly stop but rather travels around and across the surface of the rug. When borders work, they add to the impact of the rug design. And they can be an integral part of the overall design.

Borders reinforce colors that are found in the main design. By repeating those colors, you broaden the interest across the design and around the edges of the rug. Colors in the border can also provide a nice contrast to the backing. For example, a still life design with a bowl of fruit would look great with colors from the fruit and the bowl incorporated in a border. The purples, reds, greens, and golds found in the fruit would enhance the design even more. Or, if it's a traditional still life, how about an ornate mock gold frame as a border? The possibilities are endless. Let's look at just a few.

I love rugs. I love designing them, hooking them, and sharing them. I view every new rug as a challenge to do better than the last: a better design, better hooking, and better finishing.

When I start a new rug, I ask myself this question: "What will make this one special? How can I improve upon what I've done in the past?

Part of that question involves whether I will use a border as part of the overall design. Most of the time I do include borders.

When planning a rug design or using a pattern that's already drawn up, why not consider adding a border? Rug hookers often ask when to add a border and what the rules are for having a border. What I suggest is not trying to follow any set of rules but rather to let the rug dictate what looks best. Some rugs require only minimal border

cut linen

irregular hooked edge

1" linen edge

edge whipped with yarn

BORDERS INSPIRED BY WEAVING

LLarry, the Llama, 26" x 30", #6- and 8-cut wool on linen. Designed and hooked by Donna Hrkman, Dayton, Ohio, 2006.

Borders also accentuate elements of design. In *Llarry, the Llama*, I researched Peruvian fiber sources and fabrics that developed in that region. Llamas are native to Peru and used as pack and companion animals, and I wanted to tie their history into the rug design. I found some beautiful patterns and color combinations as I researched online and eventually settled on warm rusts, oranges, and creams. Llarry, whose photo I had taken myself at a llama show, was loaded with personality, so I knew that he would be suitably showcased by the bold patterns inspired by the traditional Incan borders. The top and bottom of the rug are based on a woven belt design, while the striped sides are reminiscent of blankets woven by Peruvian weavers. By combining bold elements in the border, I gave Llarry a distinctive and dramatic look. And by having the side patterns different from the top and bottom, the rug is more interesting but still not too busy.

BORDERS INSPIRED BY NATURE

Sometimes a rug needs closure—or maybe enclosure. If your design features a lot of plain background or a centralized motif, a border can finish and contain that main area, keeping it from fading away visually around the edges. In *Koi*, the main focus is the two fish circling the lily pond. They are colorful and dynamic, but the pond needs to be contained visually, otherwise the fish pond might drain away. Because the fish and lily pads are so eye-catching, a simple border seemed best. What better way to contain a fish pond that a cobblestone border? It's a perfectly natural design choice, since it's something you would see around a fish pond, and the neutral dull grays and browns are a fine foil for the brightly colored fish. To create a visual transition, I added a colorful frog in

Detail of **Koi** (See the full rug on page 90.)

one corner, adding a sense of depth and dimension, leading the eye from the surface plane of the cobblestones to the surface of the water.

CONCENTRIC STRIPES

What other types of borders work? You are limited only by your imagination. You can create a basic border using a complementary color or two, or hook a simple monochromatic border to act as a picture frame. A simple, eye-catching border is one in which you select colors from the main design and create the border with concentric stripes. In *Gargoyle*, I used black, red, and gray from the range of colors in my brother's sweet dog and simply built them out, row by row. The color combination is rather masculine, too—perfect for a male dog and for my brother's decor!

Gargoyle, 22" x 22", #6- and 8-cut wool on linen. Designed and hooked by Donna Hrkman, Dayton, Ohio, 2004.

HIT-OR-MISS

Another simple but effective design for borders is hit-or-miss. Again, the key is to select colors from the main design, then start hooking in lines around the body of the rug until you build up the border to a width you like. Keep a balance of light and dark, and space out the color arrangement. It's a quick and simple method to add a spark to the rug.

There is a lot of motion in *Red-Eared Turtle*. The swimming turtle comes into the front plane of the rug as a large central figure. The background is intentionally vague and serves as a backdrop. So the border had to be simple, yet still add a distinct frame to the image. By using a variety of closely colored and similarly valued strips, the border looks "watery" as it repeats the turtle color.

Detail of **Red-Eared Turtle** (See the full rug on page 94.)

THE BORDER IS THE RUG

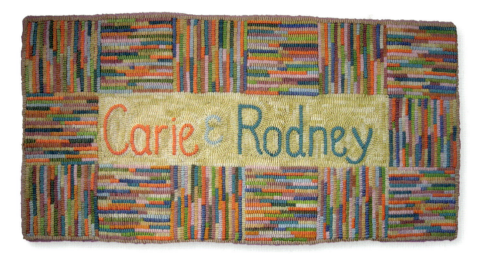

Wedding Rug, 19" x 31", #6-cut wool on linen. Designed and hooked by Donna Hrkman, Dayton, Ohio, 2007.

I drew up the rug in 6" squares, three squares down and six across, making it 18" x 36" overall. The inner section with their names is 6" by 24". I hooked the squares in stripes and drew the names in the middle, then hooked a soft yellow as the background behind the names.

I hooked a wedding rug and threw convention out the window. I designed a runner that was mostly border, with just enough space inside for the name of the couple. I knew they had chosen Fiestaware for their dinner dishes, and I thought it would be fun to hook a hit-or-miss rug with those great colors.

The finished rug is bright and fun and will be the perfect complement to display the dishes. Because I chose simple lettering for the names and used contrasting colors, they show up well, in spite of the bold, busy border. The rug works because it's balanced, even though it's not a conventional layout.

TEXT AS BORDER

Sometimes you hook a rug that needs a little extra explanation of the motif you've chosen. If you hook a rug that illustrates a poem, story, song, or nursery rhyme, the border can include text or titles. (See more about hooking letters in Chapter 6.)

THE BEAUTY LINE

A simple way to add a spark to your rug is to select a color from the rug and hook a single line, called a beauty line, around the inside of the border, separating it from the body of the rug. A bright or high-contrast color will make a nice sparkle without detracting from the design. See the red beauty line in the *Red-Eared Turtle* as an example.

Detail of **Baa Baa Black Sheep**
(See the full rug on page 40.)

TROMP L'OEIL BORDER

Detail of **Barred Owl**
(See the full rug on
page 104.)

More challenging is a tromp l'oeil border, which is French for "fool the eye." This border can be used for dramatic effect, but it can be fun and charming, too. In *Barred Owl,* I wanted to capture the handsome rugged beauty of nature in a portrait of a regal-looking owl. I drew him in the manner of a classic bust, since he's certainly king of all he surveys! So it seemed fitting that he be framed by a strong and sturdy border befitting his stature. A frame made of tree branches was perfect.

I photographed several close-ups of tree bark (which made my husband scratch his head as he watched me) and drew the border with the colors and texture of a real tree. When I hooked it, I shaded the sides of the tree branches as if the light was coming from the upper right-hand side, making them look rounded and adding a sense of three-dimensional curves. I made the left-hand sides and bottoms of the branches darker as if they were in the shade.

I also played a fun trick by hooking a woolly worm caterpillar creeping along one of the branches. I hooked him a little higher and clipped the loops to make him fuzzy. It adds a little spark, a touch of realism that breaks up the pattern of the tree bark.

Keep an open mind when using tromp l'oeil. There are endless bits of creativity you can play with to add more excitement to your borders. Don't be afraid to have fun!

IRREGULAR EDGE

Detail of **Sunflower Girl** (See the full rug on page 102.)

I enjoy creating irregular edges when they work well with a rug's design. This technique allows images to break through the lines of the border. Sometimes an image from the central body of the rug can reach across the border line into the border, and sometimes the border itself extends out past the conventional edge.

In *Sunflower Girl,* the girl's head extends slightly out of the frame and the outer lines follow that curve, accentuating her image and giving her a sort of halo, which I'm sure she deserved.

In *Blue Mermaiden,* one of the friendly seahorses swimming through the water with our star mermaiden breaks the edge on the lower left part of the rug. If you decide to extend beyond the edge of a border to make an irregular edge, it is simple to bind. I always bind my rugs with the rolled edge technique: When I finish hooking the rug, I trim the linen to 1" around, roll it over a $5/16$" cotton cord, and pin it all around with quilt pins. Then I whip it with dyed wool yarn. Where the image extends out beyond the border, I cut around that shape with a 1" border, cutting a couple of notches in the linen to ease the turn, allowing it to turn under smoothly. Then I continue to bind with yarn.

Detail of **Blue Mermaiden** (See the full rug on page 96.)

MOCK PICTURE FRAME

Detail of **Veteran's Day**
(See the full rug on
page 95.)

A more formal and traditional form of tromp l'oeil is the mock picture frame. I wanted *Veteran's Day* to look like a formal portrait of a war veteran and so I decided to create a wooden frame around the central image. I enhanced the frame image by adding a brass star in each of the four corners, and making it look more military.

The border looks like a regular wooden picture frame, hooked with light and dark variations in the colors to mimic wood grain. I mitered the inside corners as a frame would be mitered, and I hooked a single gold line around the inside edge of the border against the image so it looks like the decorative edge on a frame. It's a fitting tribute to a man who served his country.

GEOMETRIC BORDER

Detail of **Mother Goose**
(See the full rug on
page 105.)

A nother type of border style is a geometric. It can be as simple as a checkerboard of alternating colored squares or a series of concentric "pennies," but when hooking a geometric border, remember to keep it simple.

It needs to be harmonious with the body of the rug. There's nothing wrong with jazzing up the rug with a bold border, but keep in mind that geometrics are visually commanding and can overwhelm the rug if you let them. You don't want the border fighting with the main design for attention.

THE MATH

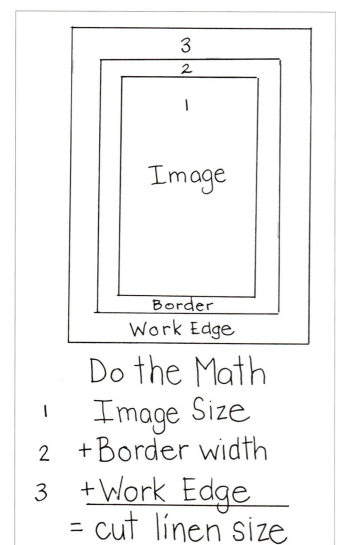

```
              3
            2
          1

      Image


      Border
   Work Edge
```

Do the Math
1 Image Size
2 + Border width
3 + Work Edge
   = cut linen size
   measure twice,
   cut once

Here's a way to calculate the size of border plus the body of the rug. If you want a 3" border, take the size of the body of the rug, say 20" x 30", and add 6" (3" per side), giving you a rug size of 26" x 36". Don't forget that you need some backing material to work with over the edges of your rug hooking frame, so add another 3" per side (6" overall), for an outside dimension of 32" x 42". That's the size you would cut your backing material for a finished rug measuring 26" x 36" with a 3" border.

Scale and proportion are important elements to consider when you're planning your rug, and that includes when you plan a border. Once you decide to add a border, you need to figure out how wide you want it to be and what elements you want to include.

I worked for 10 years in a picture framing shop, so for me, adding a border comes naturally. I calculated frame and mat sizes all day. I learned the trade from people who had been in the

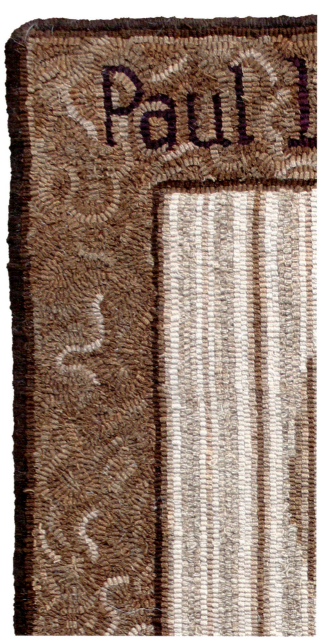

cut linen →

irregular hooked edge

1" linen edge ↑

edge whipped with yarn

business for many years, and while I was never taught a mathematical formula for determining the best width of borders around artwork, I learned to judge what looks best for different sizes.

Proportion is important when deciding your border width. Make it too wide and the main image can be dwarfed and overpowered; too narrow and the border looks like an afterthought, or like it might slip off the sides. If you want a big wide border or a skinny edge, that's ultimately your choice, and in some cases it can work. But for the most part, a large rug can support a wider border while a smaller rug demands a narrower one. A 24″ x 36″ rug should have a 3″ or 4″-wide border, while a 12″ x 16″ rug would be better served by a border of 1 $1/2$″ to 2″. Again, it's personal taste. I suggest looking at other rugs in books or magazines for ideas.

In hooking some borders, you may want to miter the corner as you hook around it, creating a 90-degree angle. One way to accomplish this is to draw a straight line from the inside corner of the border to the outside corner. This gives you the

turning point. Hook up to that line and then turn the corner to continue the line.

The last step after hooking the border is finishing the edge. Any standard type of finishing will do: rug tape, whipped yarn, braiding, or crochet. I whip my rug edges with heavy wool yarn, usually matching the color of the outside row. But contrasting colors work, too. The heavy yarn protects the outer edge of the hooking and makes a bumper against friction and wear.

Keep your mind wide open when it comes to borders. It may take a little extra work and a few more inches of linen, but the rewards are worth the effort. Sure, there are rugs without borders and they work fine, but why not explore the options when you plan that next masterpiece? You may surprise yourself.

Look at rugs created by other artists to see how they included borders in their pieces. Look at classical artwork and see how it's framed. A nicely hooked border can make a good rug look great. Don't be afraid to experiment!

CHAPTER 5

Hooking a Realistic Wallpaper Background

Backgrounds are an important element in our rugs. They perform a variety of tasks, from surrounding a motif and framing it, to providing a believable backdrop for a main character, to being a neutral foil for an image that needs nothing but calm around it. Sometimes, the background becomes a visual anchor for a rug theme, perhaps supporting a portrait or creating a sense of place for the subject.

Because backgrounds need to do all these things, I often use a mock wallpaper pattern behind my portrait subjects. It's the perfect way to create a sense of environment, a homelike setting where people naturally belong.

So when you are hooking someone or something special and you want to have a sense of place surrounding them, consider a wallpaper background. It can be as complex or as simple as you like. Stripes are easy, but imagine how rich a different type of wallpaper might be. There's no limit to what you can create!

COLOR CHOICE

Detail of **Three French Hens** (See full rug on page 98.)

One of my early rug designs featured three French hens, part of a challenge to artists to illustrate the 12 days of Christmas for a *Rug Hooking* magazine article. It was a fun project, limited to a 12″ x 16″ format. I did my research and found three heritage chicken breeds from France, each one different from the other. I drew each from the breast up, so all three were side by side, holding a length of ribbon with Christmas ornaments hanging from it. To reinforce the Christmas theme, I drew in a simple wallpaper background in rich maroon, green, and gold. It was my belief that the French hens should be properly surrounded by a rich setting, as these were clearly no ordinary chickens in a coop.

The hens, while fancy, were still not especially colorful, so framing them in a strong, solid color pattern would anchor them nicely, allow a good contrast between the color of the wallpaper and the neutral coloring of their feathers, and make a whimsical setting for chickens who normally would not be in such fine quarters.

I measured the background width, which was 16″, and calculated a repeat for the vertical lines. This pattern is one of the simplest layouts for a basic wallpaper background. It alternates two colors and uses a small line of a neutral color between them. Easy to do, yet effective. The red and green wool was mottled, giving a nice texture to the stripes and making an interesting foil for the chickens. Hooked in vertical lines, the stripes mimic a simple but elegant wallpaper.

SIMPLE STRIPES

Chloe, 16" x 16", #4- and 6-cut wool on linen. Designed and hooked by Donna Hrkman, Dayton, Ohio, 2010.

Another example of simple wallpaper backgrounds is a cat mat I hooked and sold at a local gallery. I had a sweet photo of one of our cats, Chloe, and needed to make up some easy small pieces to put in a gallery show to sell. Time was of the essence, and I quickly hooked her face, but lacked the right type of background. She was never allowed outdoors, so I chose an indoor setting with wallpaper behind her head. She was a gray and white cat with a sunny disposition, so I chose yellow and green and gray for the wallpaper backing. Again, a simple stripe in a repeated pattern, and Chloe immediately had a place to live.

ADDING SHADOWS

I was hired to create a tribute to a local poet, Paul Laurence Dunbar. The curator of his museum saw my work and commissioned a portrait of Dunbar. I was excited to create a piece like this, which would celebrate his important life and incorporate elements of his image and his poetry. Dunbar was a native of Dayton, Ohio (my hometown), and was the first African American to have his poems published in a book. He was be-friended by the Wright Brothers; his mother was their housekeeper. The Wrights helped Paul get through school and also aided him as he pursued his writing skills.

I drew the portrait and did the layout for the verse the curator had chosen. Then I set to work. I dyed the wool in sepia tones to replicate the look of the original photo. I hooked the image to my satis-faction and decided to use a curlicue border, but then I puzzled over that background. I couldn't use another textured design for the background if the border was going to be busy. I didn't want just a flat or graduated background, either, as it was going to

look stark in a monochromatic palette. I was stumped.

Looking at some historical photos of Dunbar, I decided to try a wallpaper background. I found some traditional wallpaper patterns in a book of wallpaper samples: a simple floral that might have existed in Dunbar's house. I drew up a small section on the piece and hooked it in.

It was a terrible choice. The floral background looked like cartoon word balloons behind his head. They just looked silly and detracted from the portrait. Out came the flowers.

My next thought was to use the simple stripes. I measured them out evenly across the background, chose three values of the sepia, and hooked the lines.

This pattern was better, but the spacing was wrong and the dark lines looked like prison bars. I had put an important poet in prison. So they had to come out, too. I was determined to make it work, and drew up another pattern, one that included more values of the brown sepia color. I broke the

Paul Laurence Dunbar, 25" x 36$^{1}/_{2}$", #3-, 4- and 5-cut wool on linen. Designed and hooked by Donna Hrkman, Dayton, Ohio, 2009.

stripe into a very traditional looking style: the dark lines were next to thinner stripes of various values, and the repeat took on a very believable feel of real wallpaper. Alternating the widths of the stripes made it look right.

The next step was to include his shadow on the wallpaper. This technique puts a figure immediately in front of the background, instead of far away from it. Casting a shadow is a neat trick and one that makes the image look even more realistic.

BASIC WALLPAPER LAYOUT

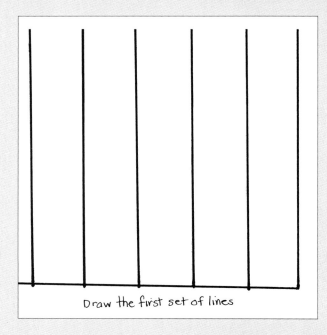

Draw the first set of lines

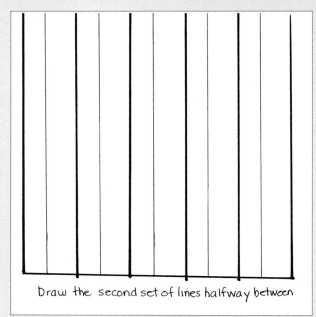

Draw the second set of lines halfway between

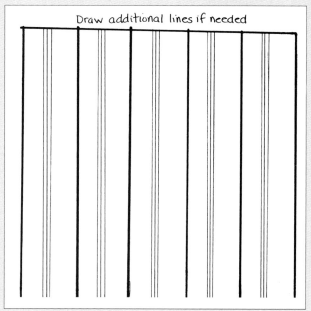

Draw additional lines if needed

Choose three colors or values: light, medium, dark. If you have a background area of 24", split the repeat into 3" sections, giving you eight repeats across the background area. Design one 3" section and repeat it across the background. A good start might be a $^{1}/_{2}$" dark stripe in the middle of the 3" area, surrounded by a $^{1}/_{4}$" of the light and then 1" of the medium. Plan, hook, repeat.

*Backgrounds perform a variety of tasks,
from surrounding a motif and framing it,
to providing a believable backdrop for a main character,
to being a neutral foil for an image
that needs nothing but calm around it.*

CASTING SHADOWS

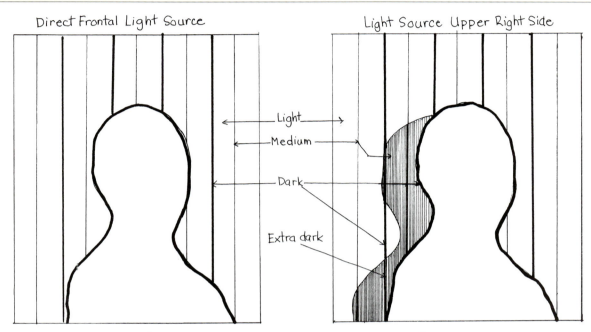

Direct Frontal Light Source

Light Source Upper Right Side

Light

Medium

Dark

Extra dark

Choose 3 values for wallpaper: Light, medium, and dark. The Light value is the majority of the wallpaper, the Medium is the center line, and the Dark value makes the darkest line.

Choose four values for wallpaper: Light, medium, Dark, and Extra Dark. The Light value is still the majority, but where the shadow is cast, the light value turns into the medium value. The medium value becomes the dark value, and the dark value becomes the very dark value.
This shift is created without outlining the shadow area; the value switches at the line along the shadow's edge

Try laying out the shadows on paper first so you can keep the pattern straight in your mind. Once you get going, it's easy to do and also a pretty quick way to fill a background space.

First, draw a simple projected line that echoes the silhouette of the person, maybe a couple of inches wide. Using this shadow line as the break between the regular wallpaper and the shaded part, you will simply bump your color or value two shades darker. So you will need two values darker than your three chosen for the stripes. That makes five values or colors. When you are hooking the stripe and get to the line that indicates where the shadow starts, switch from the wallpaper value to a shadow value that's two steps darker.

It sounds complicated on paper, but once you have your wool selected and your lines drawn, it will make sense. And the finished effect is an excellent way to show that depth and dimension on a wallpaper background.

CHAPTER 6

Adding Text

If a picture paints a thousand words, why do we need text in our rugs? Text can represent the actual lyrics of a song or lines from a poem. It can help define the meaning of an image or provide insight to the purpose of what we've chosen to hook. It can be an identifier, a signature, a title, or a phrase. The text can run through the design, be hooked around the border, be tucked in a corner as an artist's signature, or be hooked in such a way that it's a joy for the viewer to discover it. Text offers clarity and a deeper definition of what our rugs are meant to say.

Sometimes an image conveys everything we hope to communicate, but other times, an image might not be enough to illustrate our thoughts or feelings. In those situations, including some written words enhances the image. Depending on the style of the lettering, text can be as beautiful and intrinsic to the design as other elements of the design itself.

One final important use for hooking letters is signatures. The placement of your initials can be bold or subtle. Either way, all of the tips for hooking text still apply. It's up to you how you put your signature in your rug!

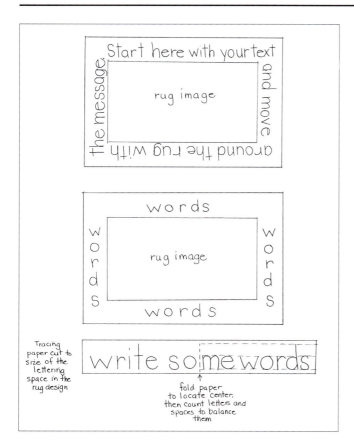

DRAW THE LETTERS

When I incorporate text into my rug designs, I keep it simple. More writing in a rug design is not necessarily better. I've found that simple fonts, simple phrases, and simple colors will convey a message much better than trying to hook entire passages. Keep these basic elements in mind when you decide to add text to a design.

- Keep it simple. It's distracting to have a lot of text in a rug. Your image should convey the main thrust of your theme; the words are there to clarify or enhance it.
- Draw the lettering in advance on tracing paper. It eliminates crowded wording and prevents you from cramping the lettering into a too-small space.
- Use the lines of your backing to keep letters straight. If you're using a script rather than printed letters, make sure the linen is even and straight and the height of the letters is consistent.
- Leave space above and below the letters as well as between the letters. Use your eye to

Hooking Letters

hook it

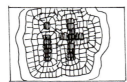
hook around it

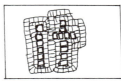
pull it out

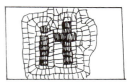
rehook it

determine the amount of space between letters, as the shape of the letters will determine how close each letter needs to be hooked to the next.

- Use a basic font. Old English lettering with serifs and varying line widths is difficult enough to read on paper; with the texture of wool, it becomes even more difficult.
- Choose a font that is legible and clear. If you choose a busy style, make sure it doesn't overpower the image.

A lot of decisions go into incorporating text. Decide the following before you get started.

- The width of the letters
- The number of rows of text
- The color or colors of the text
- Any additional treatment of the text, like outlining
- The placement of the text
- The prominence of the text (Prominent or hidden: consider that hiding words is also a powerful treatment)

After I have designed the text and calculated its placement in the rug (see the sidebar, Centering Text), I trace the letters on the backing. When the letters are on the backing, I select the size of strip I want to hook the letters with. It needs to be wide enough to be legible, but not so wide that it distorts the shape of the letter.

A TEXTING SECRET

Let me share with you a great way to keep your hooked letters as close to perfectly shaped as they can be: use placeholders! Yes, you'll end up hooking the letters twice, but the end result will be worth the effort. Here's how it works.

First I hook my letters with a #5 strip in whatever scrap wool I have to act as a placeholder. Then I hook around the letters with the background wool. Once I have completed the background around all of the letters, I then choose the color I want for the letters and cut it one size larger than the original strip. So, in this case, I'd be cutting a #6 strip.

Placeholders serve a couple purposes. For one, hooking the background around the placeholders will squish the shape of the letters. The background hooking often pushes even straight lines out of place and distorts the letters. By using placeholders, then removing the placeholders and hooking again with a slightly larger strip, you can reestablish the integrity of the line. Simply pull out the old strip, **one letter at a time**, and rehook the letter with the new slightly wider strip.

Using a placeholder for the letters also lets you shape the background as you fill in around the letters. The wider strip fills those areas more evenly and keeps the background from taking over.

I occasionally hook the second round of letters just slightly higher than the background. It makes the letters stand out more and helps them to show up better against the background.

When I incorporate text into my rug designs, I keep it simple. More writing in a rug design is not necessarily better. I've found that simple fonts, simple phrases, and simple colors will convey a message much better than trying to hook entire passages.

BORDER TEXT

Baa Baa Black Sheep, 29½" x 29½", #8-cut wool on linen. Designed and hooked by Donna Hrkman, Dayton, Ohio, 2004.

O ne of my earliest rugs was a primitive-style piece called *Baa Baa Black Sheep.* Inspired, of course, by the old nursery rhyme, I wanted to celebrate a rug hooker's fondest treasure: wool. So I created a basic sheep design and hooked four different sheep contained within a square. Each sheep had a different texture for the fleece. I loved the idea of having these simple sheep in a traditional primitive-style framework and decided that I would add the words from the nursery rhyme, with a few changes.

The wording I chose to use is "Baa baa black sheep, have you any wool? Yes ma'am, yes ma'am, three bags full." The type is basic uppercase and lowercase letters hooked with a single strip of wool in a simple font. Because the colors in the rug are dull and primitive and the backgrounds for the sheep are textured, I chose a medium value in a gold-colored wool for the words and hooked them into the light neutral color of the border.

Having a flowery text or using bright colors would be incompatible with the design style of my sheep rug. *Baa Baa Black Sheep* is primitive, it's simple, and the text has to match that look. I used a single flourish line in a different color to indicate the beginning and end of the quote so the words wouldn't run together. The writing starts at the top of the rug and runs all the way around the border.

In order to make sure it all fit, I drew the size and height of the border on tracing paper so I knew how tall to make the letters. I drew the entire phrase and then laid the pieces of tracing paper over the rug to see where to break the words to make it all fit. Once I had four separate lines, I cut the traced segments apart and copied the words onto the backing. Then it was just a matter of hooking and filling in the border around the words.

TEXT THAT MIMICS THE DESIGN

Pink Flamingo Cottage, 19" x 34", #3-, 5-, and 6-cut wool on linen. Designed and hooked by Donna Hrkman, Dayton, Ohio, 2009.

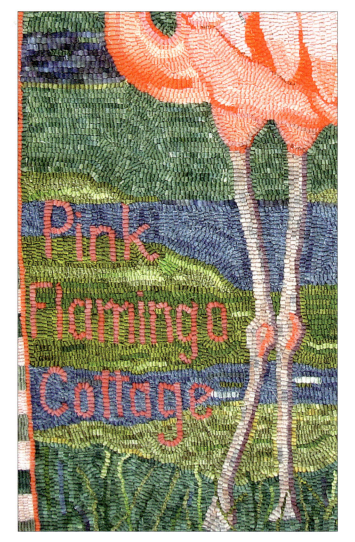

Detail of **Pink Flamingo Cottage**

In another rug project, I hooked a tall flamingo against a green background as a gift for a client's mother. His mother has a cottage by a lake, and she collects flamingo-related items and keeps them there. I incorporated the words "Pink Flamingo Cottage" into the body of the rug in the lower left corner in pink variegated wool to serve as an identifier for the piece. It customizes the design for the owner and makes it more than just an image of a flamingo. My words turn a generic flamingo into her personal flamingo.

Again, the lettering is simple and hooked with a single row of wool. It's slim and in scale with the long, skinny flamingo body. The variegated wool provides a nice warm contrast to the greens and blues of the marshy background and repeats the colors in the bird as well as the border. Everything ties neatly together.

HIDDEN WORDS

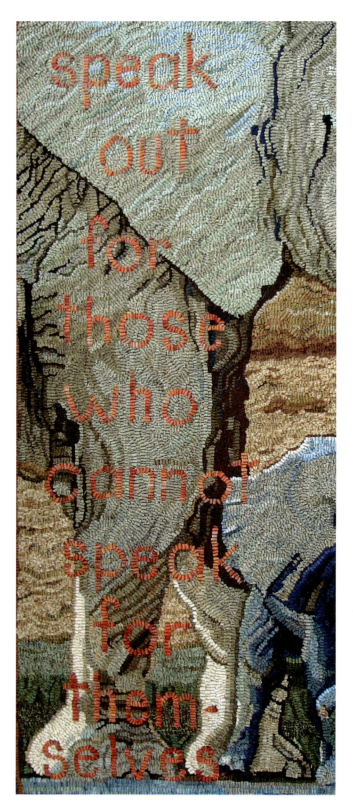

Sometimes we hook a rug that has a message. I've hooked several awareness rugs in my time, and they all include text in some form. I believe a message rug has to be clear in its purpose, so having everything spelled out is important.

Not too long ago, I saw some news stories about the near extinction of elephants in Africa. Poaching and invasion of their natural habitat had reduced the number of elephants to a horrifying new low. I tried to imagine a world without these wonderful, intelligent, loving creatures and was moved to make my own statement against their extinction. The fact that our next generation, our grandchildren, might never see a live elephant is one of my deepest sorrows. So my rug had to say so.

The lettering I chose for this rug is essentially the same simple type I use in almost all of my rugs: single line, basic letters, hooked within the design area. In this case, the lettering starts within the top border of the rug and runs down the left side of the image, ending in the bottom border. It features a quote by Jane Goodall, who has devoted her life to preserving chimpanzees. I felt her words were appropriate for elephants as well. "The least I can do is speak out for those who cannot speak for themselves."

I hooked the words in variegated wool, an orange shade that flickers with light where the wool has light spots. It stands out clearly in the deep blue border but becomes a little more difficult to read through the body of the rug. I did not wish to create a billboard, where the text dominates the image. I wanted to make the words less bold so the viewer must look closely and get up next to the rug to make them out. I want to touch the viewer, make them seek the meaning, and let it penetrate their thoughts. The image is strong and emotional, and the words need to be strong and emotional as well.

Detail of **Elephant Rug**

Elephant Rug, 26" x 37½", #3- and 5-cut wool on linen. Designed and hooked by Donna Hrkman, Dayton, Ohio, 2010.

ADD A QUOTE

Detail of **Paul Laurence Dunbar** (See the full rug on page 35.)

Paul Laurence Dunbar also has text, perhaps the most of any rug I've made. I used a little-known photo of Dunbar: his high school graduation picture. The client gave me a few lines from one of her favorite Dunbar poems. The quote is this: "Because I had loved so deeply, Because I had loved so long, God in His great compassion, Gave me the gift of song."

I hooked the quote in a basic font and laid it out at the bottom of the rug in verse form. The other text on the rug is simply his name. I chose royal purple for that lettering, as it was Dunbar's favorite color. I hooked the text at the bottom in cream-colored wool, which overlays both the bottom of the portrait as well as the bottom border. I wanted the letters to stand out clearly against the darker shades, and in a monochromatic rug, it was important to get that contrast.

WORDS AS A DESIGN ELEMENT

Detail of **Alzheimer's Rug** (See the full rug on page 92.)

Another example of text in rugs is found in my Alzheimer's rug. I felt text was necessary in this rug to make sure the message is clear. My father-in-law died with Alzheimer's disease, and I wanted this rug to be a tribute to both the victims and their families and loved ones.

The central image is the portrait of a woman with Alzheimer's disease. She has a vacant stare, a look of confusion and despair as she faces an unknown, unmanageable future. I wanted to convey her sense of loss and the feeling that she is "coming apart." I designed the image to contain the visual unraveling of her mind. I used bright colors and textures to represent the things being taken from her, which are shown in contrast to the dark, violent turmoil in the background.

The words in the border are for her loved ones, a reminder that while she may not be able to remember them, it's important to remember her. It's painful for all, but to leave her alone is unthinkable.

This rug includes more simple letters and more simple text. The letters in the border are less vivid than the words in the main design and become a secondary message in the rug. To understand the loss of all that makes us who we are, we must read the words and see what we are losing.

SCRIPT

Detail of **Olympic Spirit** (See the full rug on page 106.)

As you can see from the examples in this book, I tend to stay with the same style and type of lettering when I incorporate text into my rugs. But you should feel free to use any fonts, colors, sizes, or placement you choose. The most important tip to remember is to keep the style of lettering appropriate to the image.

In this rug, I used script instead of block lettering. I designed *Olympic Spirit* for a challenge and decided to create an image of a gymnast in a dramatic pose. I wanted to illustrate the burst of energy she created with that move. She is located to the far right edge of the rug, with her arms and legs curved behind her, and the motion of her arms has extended into long, beautiful wings. There needed to be a title on this rug, but because this piece generates so much motion, I felt that block letters would slow the movement and look clunky. So I drew the words *Olympic Spirit* in script and hooked it in. The forward movement of the lettering provides a counterbalance and keeps pace with the movement in the background and of the gymnast.

CENTERING TEXT

To figure out how to center the words, I take a piece of tracing paper and mark off the area where I want to hook letters. If it's a border, I measure the length of the area and pencil the height and width of the area on tracing paper. Then I mark the center of the area. I count the number of letters that need to go into that area, including spaces in between words.

Then I draw the letters from the middle point out to the edges. Try to think of each letter as a single element. Draw them first out to the left from the center, then out to the right from the center. Here # indicates a space. It should work like this:

1. Center the phrase at the halfway point.
Twinkle#twinkle#

little#star/How#I wonder#what#you# are!

2. Start with the letter to the left of the center first: r (the r in star)

3. Continue adding letters in reverse order:
a
t
s
#
e
l
and so on until you reach the left edge.

4. Check to make sure the letters are evenly spaced.

5. Repeat the process on the right, starting with the letter to the right of the center first.
H (the H in How)

6. Continue adding letters in order
o
w
#
I
#
w
o
n
and so on until you reach the right edge.

7. Check that the letters are evenly spaced.

8. Read the entire line to make sure each word is spelled correctly.

This method may sound a little complicated, but it works. And it keeps your letters to scale and in shape.

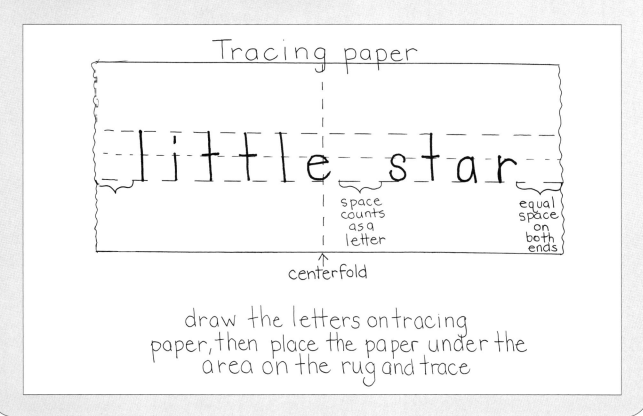

draw the letters on tracing paper, then place the paper under the area on the rug and trace

A NOTE ABOUT LABELS

I choose not to hook my signature into my rugs. It's personal preference; I never used to sign my paintings, either. It's a choice we make as rug hookers and it's up to you whether you include your initials or the date in your rug.

I am, however, a staunch advocate for attaching labels on the back. I believe rugs should be clearly labeled with information about the rug and the rug maker. It serves several purposes.

First of all, it identifies the rug and who made it. It documents the time and place where it was made and is proof of ownership.

Adding a label also makes it easier to submit the rug for shows and exhibitions. Every show or contest or gallery I've ever submitted a rug to has required a label to be mounted securely on the back. It's just good common sense to have a tag with the pertinent information attached to your rug.

What should be included in the information?
- Title of the Rug
- Dimensions of the Rug
- Name of the Rug Hooker
- Name of the Designer
- Date Completed
- Materials: Backing type, wool, yarn, etc.
- Special information about the rug theme or elements of the rug

By including this information, you ensure that the rug will be identified and documented. Odds are that the rug will outlast the person who hooked it, so the label information is an important part of history and your legacy. An heirloom should be documented for the benefit of future generations so they can understand and appreciate the hooked piece.

Rug Title

Dimensions:

Designed by:

Hooked by:

Date completed:

Foundation:

Cut of wool:

Special information:

Rug Title
In memory of my dad
1931 – 2012

When he shall die
Take him and cut him out
in little stars,
And he will make the face
of heaven so fine
That all the world will
be in love with night
And pay no worship
to the garish sun

William Shakespeare
Romeo & Juliet

CHAPTER 7

Hooking Realistic Portrait Rugs

Sunshine Girl, 16" x 16", #4- and 6-cut wool on linen.
Designed and hooked by Donna Hrkman, Dayton, Ohio, 2008.

The time may come when you want to hook a rug that features people. That rug could be whatever style and colorway you choose; stylized and brightly colored, or realistic and representational. It's all up to you. I'll share some information about how I approach realistic portrait rugs.

My specialty is representational portraiture in hooked rugs. I love being able to create that piece of art that brings a photo to life through color and texture. It's a challenge to create people's faces, and I enjoy the discipline of it all. And I gladly share what I know with anyone who's interested.

I always choose a source, usually a photograph, that is clear, large enough to provide details, and has a distinctive appeal. I have used sources that I've found online, photos of family or friends, and photos that I've taken myself. And I always ask permission to use copyrighted images.

ANATOMY OF A FACE

Your source image is your touchstone for creating a portrait that really looks like your subject. If you want your rug to be realistic, you'll need to follow a few general rules about scale and proportion in faces.

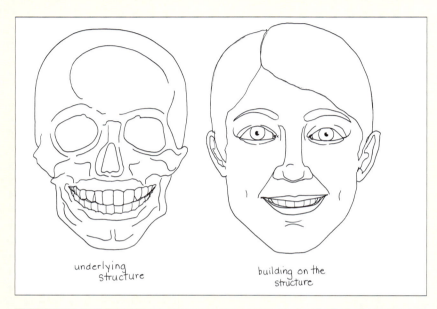

underlying structure

building on the structure

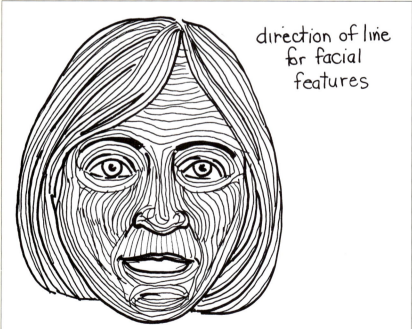

direction of line for facial features

1. The eyes are halfway between the chin and the top of the head. It seems like they are up higher, but they actually are not.

2. The bottom of the nose goes to the vertical line of the bottom half of the head.

3. Ears go from the eyes to the end of the nose. (Ears keep growing as we age, so in older folks, they may be larger and longer.)

4. The width of the eyes is roughly $1/5$ the distance between the sides of the face.

5. The eyes are one eye-width apart.

6. The width of the nose is the same as the width of the space between the eyes.

7. Lips are located $1/3$ of the way down the bottom quarter of the face.

8. Width of the lips is roughly the distance from pupil to pupil.

These elements are standard in portraiture and can be used as guidelines for creating the underlying structure of your subject.

Everything else about your rug will be determined by what your source shows you. We have a tendency to project what we know onto a subject rather than look at it and create what we actually see. Sometimes this innate tendency doesn't affect the portrait, but sometimes it does.

For example, if your source photo shows your grandfather squinting in the bright sunlight of a hot summer day, odds are good that you won't be able to see his cheery blue eyes. They'll more likely

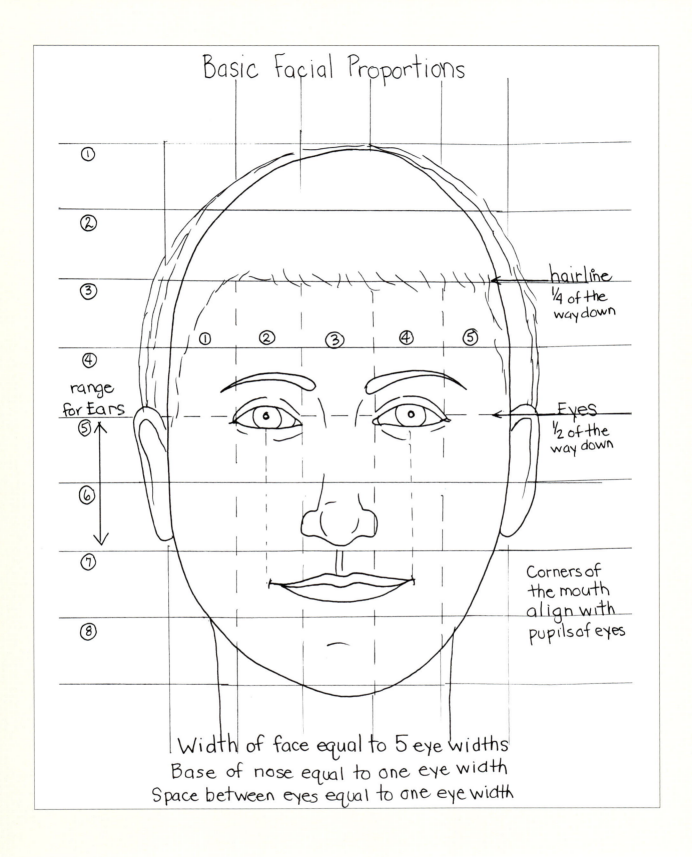

Basic Facial Proportions

① ② ③ ④ ⑤

hairline
¼ of the way down

① ② ③ ④ ⑤

range for Ears
⑤ ⑥

Eyes
½ of the way down

⑦ ⑧

Corners of the mouth align with pupils of eyes

Width of face equal to 5 eye widths
Base of nose equal to one eye width
Space between eyes equal to one eye width

show up as dark narrow lines in his face. If you try to cram blue into that space, it will look wrong, even though you know your grandfather has bright, cheery blue eyes. He's squinting! We can't see them!

Remember: Hook what you see.

It's okay if some elements are not exactly the same as the source. It's part of the nature of hooked rugs to have limits to the amount of detail you can capture, but it's still possible to get quite a

These common ways to evaluate elements in your rugs are applicable to any theme or subject, not just portraits. With portraits, when you need accuracy to create a true likeness, the devil is in the details.

lot of detail if you know how. And of course you can add personal touches to your portrait. But if you want it to be realistic, you need to follow your source as much as possible.

Transfer your design to the backing by whatever means you prefer: draw it freehand, use an enlarger/projector, use a grid process, or trace from a printed source. Make indications of shading and whatever details are important on this basic pattern layout.

My philosophy about the size of the wool strip is the same as it is in paintbrushes: use the size designed for the job. If you're painting a barn, use a wide brush. If you're painting a doll face, use a tiny brush. It's possible to render detail with wider cuts if the proportions are right for it, but even a #8-cut portrait benefits from #4- or 5-cut strips when hooking the eyes or mouth. You can hook your entire rug in a #3 cut, but you do not need to. Choose your widths based on what you need.

I do suggest staying within a range of three cuts, however. Use #3, 4, and 5 in one rug or #6, 7, and 8. Using closely related cuts creates a more pleasing texture overall.

TAKE TIME TO EVALUATE

A few tricks of the art trade apply to making rugs as well. Sometimes when we're diligently hooking away, we forget to stand back and look at the overall image. Is the color consistent? Has the shape held up or is it distorted? Does the shading belong where you've put it?

Always take breaks from your hooking to hang your rug up—the whole rug, not just what's on the frame—and look at it with fresh eyes. This new viewpoint will also allow you to stretch, get a drink, eat a snack, and take a potty break. I also suggest leaving the rug out where you can see it when you aren't working on it. This way, you see it anew and little things may pop out that you either love or hate. It's a good way to evaluate your progress.

Another way to evaluate your work is to hold your rug up to a mirror. Faces can easily be tilted slightly to the left or right, and a quick look in a mirror will make it easier to determine if they're balanced.

You can do the same thing by flipping your rug over and looking at it from the back. In the process of hooking, wool strips are condensed by the holes in the backing and expand on the top, creating a nice full-textured surface. But sometimes it's difficult to "read" detail because the wool loops are spread out against the other loops. When you look at the back of the hooking, the elements are easier to see because they're clearer and flatter.

If you get stumped at any point, try laying both your rug and your source photo upside down to compare them. Our eyes are constantly working with our brains, struggling to make connections and create images that make sense. For an example of testing this struggle, look at the work of illustrator MC Escher, whose black-and-white drawings in tromp l'oeil style defy logic. Our brains want visual images that make sense. Turning the source and the project upside down relieves our brain of those constraints. It lets us see shapes, lines, dark, and light in a non-representational way. Elements that aren't working will pop out. And once something is easy to see, it's also easy to redo!

Very big rugs should be evaluated as a whole but also in pieces. Employ this little trick to isolate a problem area. Lay a piece of paper with a square cut out of the center over your source, then lay another piece of paper with a square cut out over your rug, matching the location you isolated on your source. Compare the two areas for discrepancies and make any adjustments needed. Isolating a space will make it easier to see what's not right.

These common ways to evaluate elements in your rug are applicable to any theme or subject, not just portraits. With portraits, when you need accuracy to create a true likeness, the devil is in the details.

HOOKING EYES

Eyeballs, whether they are animal eyes or human, are all round. It's the shape of the eye that varies: that is determined by the skin around it. For example, Asian eyes are more almond-shaped because the skin of the eyelid is smooth, covering more of the eye.

Pupils are also round (except in snakes and goats and some other creatures) and they are always in the center of the iris. The eyelid, which is like an awning over a window, often casts a shadow over the upper part of the eye. The shading of the eyelids and other areas around the eye can vary a great deal, so pay attention to what your source shows you.

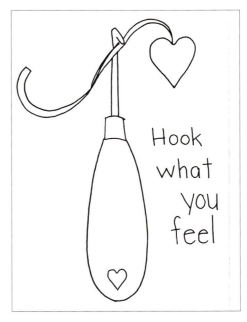

Hook what you feel

Detail of **Sunflower Girl** (See the full rug on page 102.)

HIGHLIGHTS

Highlights are a crucial part of making hooked eyes look real. The small bright dot of reflected light will transform a flat, lifeless eye into a bright, living one. Highlights on eyes indicate moisture, which indicates life.

When hooking in that highlight, I wait until the eye is completely hooked before I add the highlight. Make sure that the dot is located in the same place in both eyes. If not, the person may look googly-eyed, which is not flattering. If the face is small and has small eyes, you can still add tiny highlights by hooking in a loop from a strand of linen instead of a strip of wool.

Sleeping Baby, 14" x 18", #3- and 4-cut wool on linen. Designed and hooked by Donna Hrkman, Dayton, Ohio, 2012.

BABIES

Age is a critical factor to consider when you're creating realistic portraits. Many physical elements change as we grow older. You need to keep in mind what those changes are, and use them in conjunction with what you see in your source.

Babies and young children are smooth-skinned and often chubby. Babies don't have any hard angles; they have rounded cheeks, elbows, knees, and bottoms. They have fat fingers and toes. They have dimples in all of those places. Their hair is soft and downy, often flyaway and fine. They can have masses of soft curls or wisps of cottony lightness. Very young babies don't have long hair yet, and their hair usually follows the contours of their heads. Babies' eyes are proportionally larger in their faces because their heads are growing. Noses are usually round nubs and mouths are small and pouty. They have full, puffy cheeks and small, rounded ears, like little seashells. Think soft and round when you are creating rugs with babies.

Two Boys, 14" x 18", #4- and 5-cut wool on linen. Designed and hooked by Donna Hrkman, Dayton, Ohio, 2012.

CHILDREN

As we age, our features change. Young children still have relatively soft features, but walking and playing will define muscles in their arms and legs, their fingers lengthen, and their bodies thin out. Many go through an awkward, gangly stage where their noses look too big and their feet and elbows seem out of proportion. This needs to be reflected in your work.

Young adults have their looks in place and haven't started to show the wrinkles and graying hair of their elders. This age is actually the most difficult to hook in my opinion because there aren't as many defining features.

Older subjects are more fun to hook. Their faces are often more wrinkled, and gravity wreaks havoc with jawlines and eyelids. Smooth, tight skin starts to sag, creating extra lines and shadows. Eyelids are lower, often obscuring and shading the eye, and eyebrows, especially in men, grow with abandon until they almost take on a life of their own.

Cheeks may still be round and chubby, but look for crow's feet in the outside corner of the eye and more pronounced smile lines. Thinner people will become more angular with pronounced cheekbones, noses, and chins. Ears keep growing and seem out of proportion on some folks. Necks develop wattles and skin gets crepe-like. Teeth and smiles are different with older people; some have dentures that alter facial structure.

No matter what age does to our features, the key is to portray them as they appear in your source.

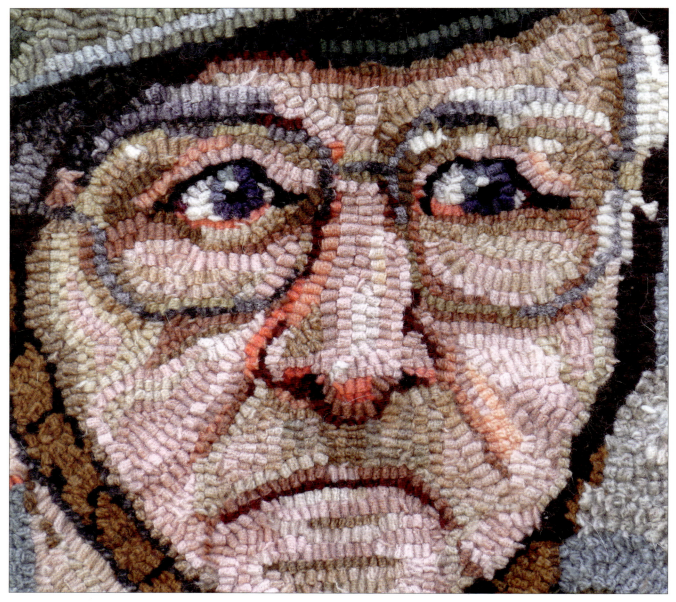

Detail of **Veteran's Day** (See the full rug on page 95.)

OLD AGE

When your subject wears eyeglasses, it's often tempting to just leave them off the image entirely. But if your subject is like me, that person may have worn glasses all of her life and wouldn't look like herself without them. My glasses are part of who I am, so they need to be included.

Your first impulse may be to hook the entire frame. When you look at photos of people wearing glasses, however, many times the image of the frames is only partial. They can reflect light, changing the color and perception of how we see them. Sometimes they make the eyes look larger. The line or outline of the frames can be downplayed so they look like part of the face and don't dominate it.

Older subjects will have different hair than younger ones. Hair becomes thinner and turns gray. Gray hair is made up of many different shades, from white to steel to charcoal. Gray hair generally starts around the face and crown, with the hair at the nape of the neck staying dark the longest. Older women may have traditional hairstyles with soft lines, and men may be gray or balding. Show thinning hair in softened colors that blend with the scalp. All of these elements add up to facial structures that represent the people in our hooked portraits.

Detail of **Sunshine Girl** (See the full rug on page 49.)

SKIN TONE

Next, we need to look at skin color. Skin colors form an amazing and unlimited palette depending on age, race, and environment. There's no such thing as "flesh color." So many components go together to make up our skin color that it's impossible to use one color for everyone. Try selecting a few base tones as a starting point for skin tone then add your shading and highlights and reflected colors to those base colors.

Choose a color palette for skin tone based on what race your subject is and the attributes of that race. Skin color varies from person to person, but it also varies based on reflection of light. The same person will appear to be one color until she stands against a painted wall, when her skin and clothing will absorb and reflect the color of that wall. These factors all need to be considered when selecting skin colors for a portrait. A subject in bright sunlight will be shaded differently from someone in cool shadow.

Look carefully at your source to see how many colors come into play. If your subject is fair-skinned, look for variations in peach, pink, tan, blue, yellow, gold, and green. If you are hooking a portrait of someone with African or other dark-skinned attributes, look for shades of brown, tan, purple, gold, blue, and red. For Mediterranean skin tones, look for olive, gold, orange, tan, and green shades. Middle European backgrounds will be paler and more pink and blue.

While these are broad generalizations, they serve as a reminder to keep your portrait relevant and realistic. It's easier to create a portrait if you know your subject and where he or she was at that moment in time. Little by little the portrait will take shape and grow into the image you want.

Remember, be open to the idea of creating a portrait in wool. Elements of color, line, proportion, and composition will all work together to make your rug come to life. You can make a rug that captures the spirit and emotion of a person, and what a great feeling that is!

OWL EYE

OWL EYE, 6" x 6", #6- and 8-cut wool on linen.

Creating the image of a hoot owl's eye isn't as difficult as you might think. It's all a matter of line and texture, applied in the right proportions. Just remember that animal eyes are not exactly the same as human eyes. While there are basic similarities, some features are very different.

The similarities are obvious. Eyeballs, whether they are human, fish, bird, or reptile, are round. The opening of the skin around the eyeball will determine the perceived shape of the eye to be oval, almond, or crescent-shaped, but remember that the eyeball itself is always round. This will help you when it comes to shading around the eyes of any animal, including people.

Not all creatures have eyelids. Snakes and fish, for example, have no eyelids. They have a thin membrane that can cover the eye for protection, but it follows the exact shape of the eyeball and does not change the roundness of it.

Through completing this sample piece, you will learn how to create a realistic-looking bit of a bird's face by combining line, color, texture, and depth.

Begin by hooking the eye. Start with the black outline around the dark round pupil. Fill in the pupil with concentric lines until the circle is filled. Leave a small gap where the highlight should appear. The highlight will make the eye look more realistic and dimensional.

Next, outline the iris (the colored part) of the eye in black. Start from the inner dark section around the outside and move up to the outer brow of the bird. This black line will define the eye and make it stand out clearly against the rest of the textures.

Hook the dark green across the upper half of the eye and the lighter green around the lower part. The owl's feathery brow extends over the eye, creating a shadow, so our owl's iris will be darker at the top and lighter at the bottom where the light hits it.

Tuck a small bit of white into the area of the pupil for the highlight.

Use the cream-colored wool to create the bright spot on the outside of the eye and follow the line across the bottom of the black outline, making small breaks for that bit of gray shading at the right side and the cinnamon color in the inside curve of the eye. Using the darker cinnamon color, outline the next ring around the white part of the eye, enclosing and encircling the socket.

Following the lines on the pattern, extend darker and lighter shades of the cinnamon-colored wool for feathers on the right side, as shown in the photo. These flatter feathers cover the owl's face. They flow from left to right.

Using the heavy textured tan and cream wool strips, outline the feathery part between the eye and the left edge of the owl's nose. The wool is thick and very textured, so be careful not to pull it apart; ease it through the holes with care. You can use the shank of your hook to widen the holes as you go. Alternate areas with the thinner textured white and gray wool to create high and low lines. Use the flat solid cream wool for the lower areas of the bird's face for more dimension.

The upper part of the owl's forehead is done with another textured wool. It's the perfect blend of black and gray and tan, but it's tricky to hook because it's loosely woven. Be sure to start at one side and work your way across the pattern lines, being careful not to crowd the rows. The beauty of this wool is the rough texture, so don't pull it too tightly. If it breaks, simply pull up the tail for the next section and keep going. It will all blend together when it's finished.

When completed, you will have a realistic study of a bird's eye. It's a lesson in line, color, contrast, and texture that you can use again and again in any animal portrait. Follow the contours, think about shape and shading, and you'll be able to make animal faces that look incredibly real.

CHAPTER 8

Awareness Rugs: Create a Rug with a Message

Detail of **Women of the Congo** (See the full rug on page 61.)

I am an artist and came to rug hooking as such. My background as an artist has given me an advantage in some respects, but in other ways I'm on the same playing field as other rug hookers.

We all love the process of creating our rugs. We love the challenges, the design, the colors, the sitting down, and the pulling of loops. There's a familiar thrill every time we pull that first row of loops, hoping this will be a good rug, our best achievement, the perfect expression of our artistic abilities. This is what we rug hookers share.

Having an artistic background does have benefits. In spite of studying art and knowing about color and design, I don't sit down to create a rug and construct it by formula. I don't say to myself,

"Hey, divide this into thirds and establish a horizon and use diagonal elements to create tension." I'm just not like that. I visualize an idea and then I sketch and check resources and then I draw a design. Then it's color planning and dyeing and a cutter and I'm off to get those first promising loops hooked in.

My rugs all start as mental images. Some come from dreams. Some are inspired by a favorite song or poem. Sometimes a photo image grabs my brain and won't let go. And sometimes I have a cause that haunts me until I grab it and pin it down and make a rug that illustrates it. Illustrating it makes it real. Illustrating it makes it visible to others. Making it real raises awareness.

SELECT YOUR CAUSE

Selecting your topic or cause should be the easiest part of creating an awareness rug because it will be something important enough in your life experience to be an automatic choice. The cause will be different for everyone. My causes are the result of my own experience, and yours will be also. What's important is that you pull deeply from what you know and express it in your rug.

Size doesn't matter. You can get a message across without creating a billboard. My *Alzheimer's Rug* is about 18″ x 24″, and yet the message is loud and clear. Work in a format that is comfortable for you and that allows you to express your thoughts and feelings without constraint. If it's a giant rug, then make it so. If it's something you want to contain within a smaller area, that's fine too.

I begin any new design with drawings and research. I check my own resources of photographs and see which I can use. I ask people to pose for me as models for future projects. I also search the Internet for copyright-free images when I need one.

I suggest you compile a collection of images and thoughts and start a folder for an awareness rug. This will keep your ideas and impressions in one place when you're ready to build your design plan. When you feel like you have a good base for your design, use your favorite technique to compose your design. Whether you use an overhead projector, grid, or a printing shop, or make your drawing freehand, get something on paper that you feel good about. It doesn't have to be perfect, and you should be flexible at this point about keeping your options open. If you intend to use lettering, figure out where you want it to go.

DOES IT NEED TEXT?

Some messages don't need words; the image conveys all that needs to be understood. But in some cases, the words are an integral part of the image and are necessary to get the message across.

When incorporating words into a rug, consider how you want them to be seen. You can put the writing around the edge of the rug within a border. Where you start the text and end it should make sense as it works around the border. Remember, most of us read left to right and the lettering should follow one direction. Think about placement and legibility as you lay out your lettering. For more tips on how to add text to your rug, look at Chapter Five.

If you are including the words within the body of the rug, figure out where they will be most effective. I like to have my words become part of the rug by making them low contrast in color and design. I don't want my rug to be like a commercial advertisement, where the lettering is bold and overt. I want the design to be first and the words to

be an intrinsic part of it. In the *Elephant Rug,* the quote starts within the top frame and extends vertically down through the image. The color sets it apart from the rest of the design, but it isn't in high contrast. I want the viewer to seek out the phrase and see it as part of the whole image.

I used the same technique in *Women of the Congo,* where the phrase at the top of the rug is very low contrast. The stark, blood-red words at the bottom of the rug are more emphatic and easier to read. They are meant to convey the horror of the Congo genocide whereas the quieter message at the top is one of hope. Those quieter words are the balance for the horror.

In other cases where I have used words in the borders, it's been to keep the image clear. In the *Alzheimer's Rug,* a lot of visual activity is happening. Having the words within the image would be more disruptive. This image does have a lot of power as it is, but the purpose is to show how Alzheimer's affects the loved one and the family.

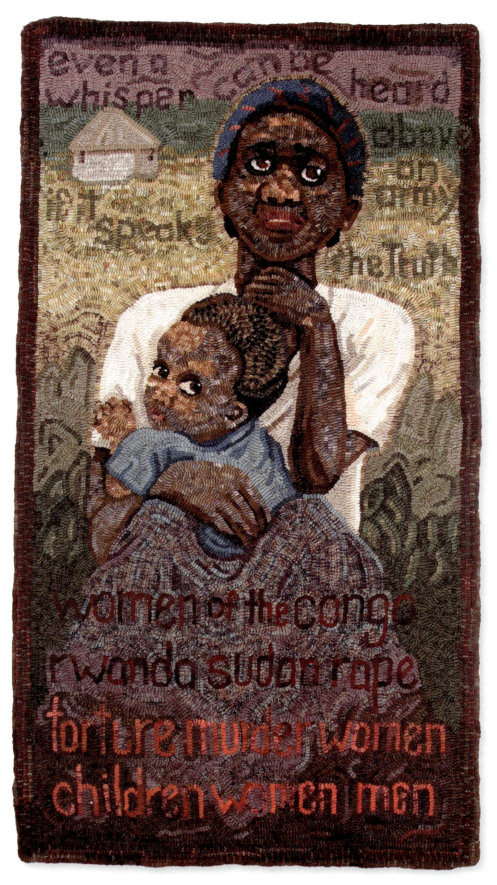

Women of the Congo, 26" x 52", #5-, 6-, and 8-cut wool on linen.
Designed and hooked by Donna Hrkman, Dayton, Ohio, 2005.

Abuse, 22" x 22", #3-, 4-, and 5-cut wool on linen.
Designed and hooked by Donna Hrkman, Dayton, Ohio, 2013.

In *Abuse*, which has been rendered as a Polaroid photograph, the lettering appears in the border. The woman in the photo has been abused, but her condition is not evident enough without the addition of words. Physical and emotional abuse go hand in hand, and she represents the victims of both types of abuse. She looks weary and devoid of emotion because she has been reduced to the point of detachment.

I wanted to raise awareness about violence against women with this rug. I had a coworker years ago who was a victim of abuse. I didn't know it until she confessed to me in private. She was able to get away from her husband and start her life over, but she suffered for years, unable to get free. She had no support, no one to talk to, and seemingly no way of escaping. She was desperately unhappy, but kept a facade of normalcy that kept her secret safe.

In order to show the effects of this brutality, I included the words in the borders of the photograph. The primary sentiment is this: "If you hear it often, you start to believe." Abusers do their best to demean and denigrate their partners. They strip them of their self-confidence and make them dependent. Abusers manipulate and injure their victims until there is no shred of dignity left. The women don't leave because they are afraid—afraid their families will be injured or even killed, afraid they won't be able to make it on their own, afraid they aren't worthy of being saved.

The words had to help convey that message. Stark, simple letters do it best.

COLOR

Your choice of colors will help convey your message. Think about what your goal is and plan your palette accordingly. In *Women of the Congo* (page 70), I chose a beautiful natural setting of the Congo's landscape behind the woman because I wanted her to be safe and in her own place. But at the bottom of the rug, I used dark colors and blood-red letters to convey the horror of her story.

In *Alzheimer's Rug* (page 68), the woman is portrayed in realistic colors, but the background is dark and threatening, with diagonal lines slashing across the rug. Diagonal lines suggest turmoil and unrest, and she has a future that is dark and uncertain. Using bright, cheerful colors would have confused the image and would not have made sense.

In *Abuse* (page 62), a black-and-white color scheme sets the tone for a woman who has become colorless and invisible. I chose not to use actual colors because I wanted to minimize the effect of her bruised and bloodied face and focus more on the sadness and despair in her eyes. The eyes are rendered in green, the only color in the portrait. The lettering is done in red for the main quote, while the words that her abuser uses are in shades of gray. They are part of the image, but not as bold as the quote.

Using color to put your message in context is important. Think about what your image is trying to say, and choose colors, or sometimes a minimalized color palette, to make it work.

Colors set the mood and tone of a rug. Bright, cheerful colors are happy and fun. Bold primary colors are solid and vibrant, lively, and vigorous. Dark colors are somber and can be dulled down to indicate a quiet or sad mood. High contrast between colors can create tension and unrest, and a contrasting color can make an element stand out.

SOURCE PHOTOS

As you plan your awareness rug, remember that you are delivering your message visually. Combining text and color is part of the delivery, but finding a strong image will bring it all together.

Another rug I created has important messages of its own to share. *Veteran's Day* was inspired by a rug hooking challenge held annually at the Sauder Village Rug Hooking Week event. Each year there's a challenge, which I usually dismiss at first and later decide to do. This particular challenge was "Happy Holidays," and I knew the majority of rugs would be Christmas or Halloween or Thanksgiving. I wanted something different, and my choice was Veteran's Day.

Most of us, if not all, have either had a family member or friend in the military or have even served in the military ourselves. It's something personal, yet the importance of service connects millions of people. My rug is a tribute to those who have served, but it also contains other messages.

The soldier in the rug is Joseph Ambrose. He was a World War I veteran. His photo is in the public domain, and the original shows him standing as I portrayed, but there is a crowd of people behind him. I eliminated the clutter of the crowd and focused on him. He represents the proud soldier who served his country, the traditional man who has saved his uniform and pulled it out of mothballs for a tribute parade or Veteran's Day memorial service. The uniform has holes in it, the epaulettes are sprung up without buttons to anchor them down. The sleeves are frayed and worn.

But he wears it proudly. The medals he earned are still attached, and the belts and sashes are there. He's wearing the helmet, but the leather chin strap is cracked and worn. He is standing at attention and he's proud, but there is something else in his eyes. There is a sense of profound loss.

Some messages don't need words; the image conveys all that needs to be understood.

Detail of **Veteran's Day** (See the full rug on page 95.)

He lost friends, compatriots. He's holding a folded flag, too, which was taken from his son's casket, the son who died in Korea. He's proud of his service, but he knows the bitter sadness of loss, what war takes from us.

I replaced the people in the original background with a stormy sky. The diagonal lines of the clouds represent unrest and disharmony. I felt that a sunny sky or a sky filled with puffy clouds would have betrayed the message. The rest of the background is tranquil and still, an autumn day, a peaceful landscape. This is, perhaps, where Joseph will find his rest.

WHY A MESSAGE RUG?

So many elements go into creating a rug with a message. The rug becomes the vehicle for your emotions and beliefs and ideas.

I ask one thing of each of my students: I ask that during their rug hooking careers they make one rug that is an outreach, a message, an awareness rug. It can be a rug that raises awareness about a cause that means the most to them. It could be for an animal shelter, a library, autism, poverty—whatever strikes a chord in their heart.

And when they make that rug, I ask them to share it. Their rugs hang on loan or as a donation in the local school or library or women's center or retirement home. Their rugs present a message that people see and relate to, and the rugs make people stop and think. These are messages that need to be shared.

Try an awareness rug. You will feel good about having done something, about creating a work of art that has a deeper meaning and connects to others. It will give you a sense of having done something pretty wonderful. Really wonderful.

WHAT IF?

A few words about inspiration and imagination

Students always ask me this:

"Where do you get your ideas?" And I always answer the same way: from my imagination. I never stop dreaming.

My rugs are my way of sharing myself. I want the rugs I create to draw the viewer in, make them think, connect with them at some level. Sometimes an image will be attractive, but when studied, more layers of meaning come through.

What do you want your rug to say?

Is it a decorative piece, a design to complement the decor? Or do you want to create something with a message? Do you want to mark an occasion or pay tribute to someone? Or maybe you just want to hook something fun.

Use Sources

Whatever you decide to hook, have a few good sources on hand, like photos or drawings. These will provide a solid framework to build on. Once you have that foundation, have fun adding the details. Be confident in your design and your work.

I tell students to ask this simple question: *What if. . . .?*

What if pigs could fly?
What if flowers had faces?
What if your dog wore a hat and glasses?
What if dragons were real?
What if kittens grew on trees?
What if houses were made of candy?

Absurd questions can lead to wonderful, artistic rugs. Inspiration and creativity can lift us right up and out of our same old ruts and ignite new ideas and images. Why not create something from your own imagination? I know that you have ideas and mental pictures lying around in your brain that are begging to be brought to life.

I have a wooden trunk that is stuffed with drawings, sketches, and notes. There are ideas for rugs in there that I haven't yet had the time to make, but the ideas are sound. They are safe in the trunk until I find the time.

Every day I think about what my next rug should be and my "to-do" list continues to grow. I'll get to those ideas eventually. The key is to keep imagining and asking, "What if. . .?"

CHAPTER 9

Limited Color Palettes and Monochromatic Rugs

In spite of being an artist who loves color, I often feel compelled to let go of that love and look toward a different way of expressing my creativity. Whether my subject will be represented in a black-and-white rug, a sepia-toned monochromatic, or a rug with a limited color range, I see this type of rug as a challenge and an opportunity to explore the possibilities as an artist and a rug hooker.

For the sake of brevity, I will refer to these rugs as monochromatic. Monochromatic means "one color," and black-and-white rugs by definition are not a color at all. But rather than repeating "limited color palette," I will say monochromatic. It's just simpler that way.

Most of my monochromatic rugs are portraits. I seldom hook landscapes, and I haven't hooked any still lifes or geometrics in ages; portraits are my genre of choice. I have done rugs in black and white, sepia, blue, and green monochromatic palettes, and every time I feel like I've learned a little something more.

A monochromatic palette creates the need for other design elements to step up and give the image impact. Color is such an important part of the equation in rug hooking that we often rely on it to carry the weight of the image. But when we eliminate colors, we open the door for greater creativity. Other design elements come forward in greater strength, such as contrast, line, contours, values, and depth. The design becomes more important because the components have gotten stronger. And it's a great thing!

Where do you begin to choose what to hook in a single color range? How do you decide what works in a monochromatic palette and what does not? The image you want to hook will help you decide. The easiest approach is to choose a source that already exists in a monochromatic format, like old photographs or prints. Many rug hookers who create monochromatic rugs work from a historical photo, a pencil or charcoal drawing, or a black-and-white picture from the family album.

If you want to use a source that is in color, you can alter it to a black-and-white or monochromatic palette.

- Use a computer to print the photo on a black-and-white printer.
- Take the printed or digital image to a print shop and ask them to convert it.
- Find an app or software program that allows you to upload a color photo and select posterizing, oil painting, black and white, sepia, or watercolor.

When I start a new monochromatic rug, I work with a minimum of eight values. A color value is the measurement of the lightness or darkness of a color. Contrast is the difference in degree of light and dark values, and gradation is the degree of lightness and darkness relative to the shading of the image or subject. Close values will flatten a shape, whereas high contrast values give a more defined shape. A good contrast range will give your design depth and dimension, and using a wide range of light, medium, and dark values will make your image richer and more visually textured.

Close values will flatten a shape,
whereas high contrast values give a more defined shape.
A good contrast range will give your design depth and dimension.

MONOCHROMATIC RUGS

T he woman who commissioned *Paul Lawrence Dunbar* asked me to use a black-and-white graduation picture as the source but hook it in warmer tones of brown.

I dyed eight values of one color dye using dye spoons that ranged from 1 teaspoon to $1/128$ teaspoon. This range gave me a very dark brown all the way to a barely shaded white. I added a pure white value of undyed wool for highlights. This range corresponded to the range of grays in the photo very well and gave me a simple translation from image to rug. The photo was not high in contrast, as some old photos tend to be, but I was able to darken and lighten some areas to create more contrast as needed.

I hooked the border with small curlicues. I put Dunbar's name at the top in the only different color of the rug, a deep purple, which was his favorite color. Because the lettering of the poem covered both light and dark areas at the bottom of the rug, I chose a medium value for the letters so they would show up on both backgrounds.

Details of **Paul Laurence Dunbar** (See the full rug on page 95.)

Detail of **Native American Boy** (See full rug on page 91.)

This photograph grabbed me and wouldn't let me go, so I had to hook it. I followed the same procedure I had used for *Dunbar:* dyeing eight values in chocolate brown. The dye holds its own for the most part, but changes in water temperature and other factors often cause this dye to split, creating variations in the color, especially in the midranges. This tendency is actually appealing to me as it makes a more natural-looking blend of values. The result is areas of the rug where the basic purple/brown gets a little bit of gold in it.

Once again, I started with the face and eyes first and worked from there. The contrast in the original photo is quite strong, making it easier for me to translate the values. The weak part of the photo is the boy's hair, which gets less in focus as it moves down the boy's front. I had to improvise the line and value a bit because the image was fuzzy, but it wasn't hard to interpret.

The background for the Native boy is a squiggly graduated value type of hooking, which starts out dark at the bottom and gets lighter in bands of value to the top. It's not busy, and the visual texture is smooth and even.

What makes this rug so strong is the degree of contrast between the lightest lights and darkest darks. It's crisp and sharp, and the emotion on the boy's face shines through clear as day.

MONOCHROMATIC WITH COLOR

Detail of **Sunflower Girl** (See full rug on page 102.)

She's another commissioned rug, and one that was a lot of fun to create. She's not a true monochromatic rug, either, as she is hooked in black and white with color accents. I gave her blue eyes and hooked the sunflower in true colors, just to liven up the image and make it more fun.

The value range on the little girl is fairly sharp and contrast is good. She's wearing a smocked dress and that area gets busy with patterning, which is nice. The background is very busy, but I kept the values close together so it stayed neutral and made her face and arms clear and important in the composition. Adding the color doesn't detract from the integrity of the design; it adds to the design in a playful way. I enjoyed capturing the look of delight on this child's face as she reaches up to touch the golden petals.

The background is very busy, but I kept the values close together so it stayed neutral and made her face and arms clear and important in the composition.

USE COMPLEMENTS

Detail of **Blue Mermaiden** (See full rug on page 96.)

When you make a monochromatic rug, it can be fun to choose a color that is out of the ordinary: not sepia, not black and white, but a *color*. When I was asked to hook the *Blue Mermaiden* as part of a color challenge, I had to go for it. Blue is a favorite of mine, and I immediately thought of creating a mermaid underwater.

I chose a single blue dye and dyed eight values from dark to light. I added a white piece for highlights and laid out the design on backing. The design part was easy and the rug was fun to hook and went rather quickly.

When hooking in a single color, you sometimes need subtle blending to make areas realistic. Shad-

ing with the different values is not difficult, it just takes some thought and consideration. The face of the mermaid is subtle in its shading—just pale blues in gradual shading. But that shading makes her look lovely and smooth under the waves.

I broke the mermaid's tail down into segments and shaded it top to bottom to look like it's bending fluidly underwater. The added complement of orange is an unexpected twist, assuring that the seahorses stand out against the blue. The mermaiden's eye is also orange as is her starfish hair barrette, so that complementary color moves across the rug. The seahorse on the outer edge also breaks the plane of the border edge, protruding a bit off the side. Those small touches give the image even more movement.

TRUE MONOCHROMATICS

Detail of **Steampunk Polly** (See full rug on page 100.)

I created this small rug after hooking the big *Steampunk Reverie* rug. I wanted a more focused rug that featured another Victorian woman who exemplifies the Steampunk look. This particular shade of green has an aged quality to it, so I dyed it in eight values and was off and running!

The contrast in this rug is simple and yet clearly defined. Her embellishments make her stand out, but they don't dominate the image because she has such great presence. This rug is also a true monochromatic, as there are no other colors present.

The range of values will determine how dramatic or how soft your monochromatic rug will be. It's up to you where you place the drama in a piece when color is restricted and which design elements you push to the forefront. Adaptability is the strength of monochromatic rugs.

CHAPTER 10

Hooking a White Rug, and What Came Next

I teach a lot of workshops, and sometimes a class will have a specific theme. I was planning a workshop about the importance of line as a design element in our work, and I wondered what it would take to show how important line can be to rug hooking designs.

In the middle of the night I realized that I would have to make a drastic change in how I approach design. The color we use in rugs is in the lines themselves. Lines equal wool strips in rug hooking, so with every strip or line, we apply color to the composition. Where would we be without them?

Where indeed?

I had a flash of inspiration. What if I removed color completely from the equation? What if a line alone could define an image? It was as if I had been struck by lightning.

I immediately pulled out my materials and drew a pattern of a fat goldfish with a long, flowing tail.

I wanted an image that would be well defined in terms of recognition and interesting inherent textures. A fish has a wonderful variety of textures because of its scales and fins and eyes. I not only drew the outline of the fish, but also all of the elements of it. I drew the lines that formed the fins and tail, the lines around the eye, and the textured lines of the scales on the fish's body.

I drew the fish's tail to extend outside the right side of the frame. It acts as a lead-in from the outside to the inside of the composition. Once I had everything drawn in, I got the wool ready.

I chose Dorr white wool. I had washed it so it was nice and tight. I cut a variety of strip sizes so I could make good use of the different textures Dorr makes. I mostly cut #3 strips, but I also cut #4 and 5 strips for the fins and tail, which would have wider and flatter elements than the fine scales on the fish body.

LOOP HEIGHT CAN ADD DETAIL

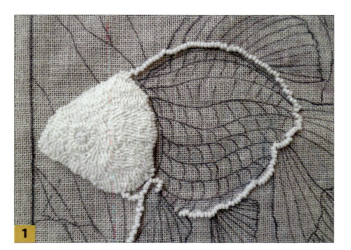

First loops

Adding the fins

Notice the ridges

I hooked the entire outline of the fish body, making sure it was hooked fairly high. That outer edge line defined the shape of the fish and provided the stopping point for the rows that would run front to back. When that line was in place, I started to fill in. **(1)**

First I hooked the eye, raising the loop for the pupil and then hooking the rest of the eye lower. Then I hooked the line around the eye higher than the middle area. It was taking shape!

The head was next. I hooked around the eye, slightly lower than that row around the outside edge of the eye. I began filling in the rest of the head, hooking as low and as uniformly as possible.

Then I moved to the body. I had drawn lines on the pattern to indicate where the scales formed across the body. Hooking horizontally across the fish, I kept the loops low on the main part and raised a single loop when I crossed the line. The next loops were low again until I reached the next line. I hooked from the top of the fish to bottom, and the lines began to stand out as they formed the rows of scales.

The fins called for wider cuts to show the broader areas between the thin ridges of the spines. I used #4 and 5 cuts to fill in the spaces where the fins were fanned out and #3 cuts for the spines. I hooked the tail in the same fashion, with flatter, wider cuts for the fin areas and narrower cuts pulled higher for the ridges. The tail has a slight bend as it flows around, and I hooked the lines to show that. The tail extends beyond the frame of the piece, which helps the image stand out and breaks the rectangular edge. **(2, 3)**

The rug began to come together as an actual image, even though it was hooked without color. It was not necessary to define the shape and texture with various colors, and by choosing a variety of different widths and heights of loops, I discovered that I no longer had to rely on color to show where the parts of the fish were different.

HOOKING THE BACKGROUND

4 The tail extends beyond the edge

5 Finished **White Fish** rug

The next challenge was hooking the background. It had to show off the image of the fish without detracting from it or interfering with it. Creating the contrast would have been simple if I had been using color, but I had to complete the challenge without compromise, and that meant all-white wool.

My first idea was to hook the background area from the underside of the rug. I figured that having the flattest possible surface would allow the image of the fish to stand out the most. So I flipped the piece over and began to fill in around the fish from the back side of the rug. It wasn't difficult to do, and after a few rows I flipped it over to see how it was going.

I didn't like it. The rows were tidy enough, and flat, but the spaces between the rows were unattractive and distracted from the flow of the white wool. When we hook from the top, the loops all blend smoothly together and you can't see the empty rows between the hooked lines. But from the back side, those empty spaces were obvious

So I took that out and started again from the top front of the rug. I hooked very low loops around the fish, careful to keep them shorter than the raised outline of the fish. Building out from the fish, I hooked smooth, even rows with low loops. There

was enough contrast between the higher lines that defined the body of the fish and the low lines of the background. I finally got the look I was after.

To finish hooking the top and bottom of the design, I drew two sets of raised lines to create a simple border. I hooked those lines with wider strips to make a flat, finished line to close off the area. The sides of the rug were left without a border, and the fish's tail extends out from the right side, breaking the visual plane. **(4, 5)**

FINISHING THE RUG

The rug was ready to be finished, so I trimmed off the excess linen and then turned the edge over cotton cording and whipped it with a wool/alpaca blend yarn that matched the white wool and had a slight sheen to it.

I was very pleased with the results. I had accomplished my goal of creating a rug with the image formed by line and texture only, without any color. The effect is striking and unusual.

But that led me to ask another question: What if I added color back into the equation, without relying on strips of dyed wool to build the design?

GOING BEYOND WHITE

The wool strips we use to hook define where the color goes. Where the strip ends, the color ends. What if I applied color via dye to a white rug surface and let it extend beyond the lines of the hooked rows? What would it look like, and would it even work? How would the color look without the lines to form it?

I had to find out.

I was so eager to try this idea that I quickly hooked up a little 3″ x 4″ mat on linen with a simple fish face in profile for the image. I hooked it with #3 strips, all white wool, and with a few areas of raised loops for texture. **(6)**

When I had the mat all hooked, I filled a bowl halfway with hot water and dissolved some Synthrapol in it. Synthrapol is a wetting agent used to help water penetrate wool to prepare it for dyeing. I figured it would be the best way to soak the mat thoroughly and get it ready to take the dye. I wanted to be certain that the wool piece was well saturated and able to absorb the dye.

While the little fish was soaking, I prepared the dyes. I wanted to keep the colors fairly transparent, like a watercolor painting. (If I wanted the colors to be darker at some point, I could either apply several layers of light color or increase the amount of dye in the solution. But for the first run, I wanted to start with a minimal amount of color.) I wanted the color to flow over and across the hooked rows without overwhelming the delicate textures of the hooked lines.

I chose four colors of Pro Chem dyes to work with. They are the same powdered acid dyes I use to dye my wool yardage. I like the pure chroma of these dyes, and I wanted the colors to be clean and

6

White sample before painting

bright. I set out four glass measuring cups and added $1/4$ teaspoon of each color to the cups: red, yellow, blue, and green.

I dissolved the dye with boiling water, filling the cups to the 1 cup line. I stirred the solutions to make sure the dyes had dissolved completely. I laid out a piece of aluminum foil to put the wet mat on so it would not bleed onto anything.

I used a sable watercolor paintbrush with a rounded flat edge so I would have good control of the dye color. I dipped the brush into the first color and carefully applied the dye to the fish face. The dye was thin and was absorbed quickly into the surface, but I wanted to be sure that it would reach deeply enough into the loops that no white wool would show through. I applied the different colors, sometimes going over the same area a few times, letting the colors blend and mix right on the surface of the mat. In areas where I wanted deeper color, I simply applied more dye. I moved the brush across and over the hooked rows, allowing the colors to blend with each other.

7

Painted sample, wet

8

Painted sample, dry

When I had covered the entire area with dye, I took a wider brush and applied a mixture of citric acid dissolved into warm water. Citric acid is a setting agent that keeps the dye from fading or bleeding when the wool dries. I rinsed out the brushes and lifted the wet mat off the foil and onto a folded paper towel. I poured the remaining dye solutions out and washed out the measuring cups. I took the mat outside to dry on the porch.

At first, when the mat was still soaking wet, I was a little disappointed in the surface. It was fuzzy and blurry looking. **(7)** The brush had loosened up the surface layer of wool fiber, making it look less defined than I wanted. But as it dried, the lines and loops tightened up and the image was sharp and clear again. **(8)**

I knew that for long-term projects I would have to find out how to set the color. The citric acid works when the dyed wool is heated and I had only applied it and let it dry. I called a lab tech at Pro Chem and told her what I was experimenting with. She said it sounded like a fascinating process and suggested that the wool mat be heated over steam for at least 30 minutes to preserve the integrity of the color.

With small pieces, I can see that the heating/steaming process would not be difficult. It would be more challenging for larger rugs, but I see the hand-painting process as something that would work best on small rugs anyway. I intend to try a variety of sizes and images in the future to see what the limitations might be.

I am thrilled with the results of my two experiments. It was a challenge to create an all-white rug that is beautiful and artistic, and I can see many more possibilities for the technique. I essentially took a major element (color) out of rug hooking and then put it back in a different way.

I asked myself a question and went about looking for the answer. Why be satisfied with the status quo in hooking? Why not step back and look at rugs in a new way? Don't be afraid to ask, "What if?" and then follow through.

Rug hooking is art. We can choose to create the same rugs over and over, or we can look at our work and think of another way to be creative. You cannot fail; you can only try different approaches and learn from what you do. I know that hooking a white rug is one concept I will be exploring further, and painting with dye is another. There are more rugs to be made!

Rug hooking is art. We can choose to create the same rug over and over, or we can look at our work and think of another way to be creative. You cannot fail; you can only try different approaches and learn from what you do.

CHAPTER 11

Expanding Creativity

Steampunk Reverie (For a larger view, see page 101.)

Steampunk Reverie is a collection of rug hooking techniques and concepts. She is a compilation of rug hooking elements and goes a bit beyond traditional rug hooking in several ways. What I love about this rug is how well all of the different elements came together to create a wonderful rug I'm proud of.

Many of the different creative techniques outlined in this book came together in this rug. It's a portrait, it contains added textures, there is a realistic background and a slightly fantastic one, and it has depth, shading, and a special border design. This rug is a great example of the possibilities for creativity, innovation, style, and technique.

I fell in love with Steampunk a while ago. It's an art movement that came about in the 1980s—it's a blend of the Victorian Age meeting the Industrial Age. I love the motifs and colors, the ingenuity and the cleverness, the drama and the style—all rolled into an uproarious mishmash of gears and gauntlets, cogs and corsets, feathers and fog. It's a flashback to movies like *20,000 Leagues Under the Sea* or the 1960s television series *Wild Wild West*. The elements of Steampunk include (but are not limited to) gears, flying machines, steam pipes, goggles, top hats, watches, corsets, feathers, ravens, and fantastic contraptions. Steampunk is jewelry, clothing, architecture, sculpture, and even food. There are Steampunk cakes and cookies, Steampunk earrings, necklaces, and bracelets, Steampunk design and clothing. It's an art movement that is energetic, boisterous, and fun.

When I first thought about creating a Steampunk rug, I knew it had to be bold and different. I wanted to make a portrait, so I found an old photo of a young Victorian woman wearing an elegant gown and an incredible hat. What I love most about the photo is the woman's expression. Goofy hat or not, she owned the look. If she could pull that off, she could handle anything I dressed her in.

I drew up the initial design on tracing paper. She was slightly smaller than life size, and I drew her from the waist up. I wanted to give her detailed facial features and enough room to include a variety of Steampunk imagery around her. The Steampunk style is busy, cluttered, and full of movement, but I wanted the rug to have breathing space and some areas of visual relief.

The original drawing includes Charlotte, the star of the rug, with a large clockface behind her. I modified her hat and tilted it rakishly to one side, adding some big roses, gears, and pearls draped from the brim. The original had did not have a feather; I added a big ostrich plume to balance everything out. The design has gears galore, from under the brim in her hair to her shoulders and down across the middle of the rug behind her.

I created Charlotte's face in one sitting and was pleased with the outcome. I never changed anything about it. The hair and hat were next, and then I moved to hook her bodice. In the original photo, the dress is a solid color with flat pleats and trim. I decided to break up the area by hooking a floral texture, suggesting a brocade. It makes a more interesting foil for the raven in front of it and by adding highlights and shadows, the bodice is more realistic. I kept the large leg-o-mutton sleeves solid, but with all the highlights and shadows in the bulky folds, they are still quite effective.

It was important to include the play of light across the bodice. The light reflects across the front of the dress from one side to the other, establishing a horizontal movement that includes the gears on both sides of the background. This horizontal movement is important because the rug has a strong vertical movement, and this movement in the opposite direction balances that vertical force.

Charlotte's skirt lies in swooping folds, and I was careful to match the highlight colors to those on her big sleeves. The light source had to be the same to make the dress look natural. The lace on her collar and cuffs was a challenge, as hooking lace requires its own technique. It's necessary to

Detail of **Steampunk Reverie**

Detail of **Steampunk Reverie**

hook the negative space of the holes and pattern in the lace and hook the lighter parts around those dark areas, creating patterns. And where the lace lies over the dress, those cut-out areas are blue; but where the lace lies across her hands, the holes are skin toned. Just a small detail, but it lends to the visual credibility. Using highlights and shadows made the whole process easier.

One change I made was in the color of the raven in her hands. It was meant to be stainless steel in the beginning, but with all the other cool colors, it would have been boring and could have disappeared in the image. So I switched to a copper raven, shading him in warm tones and connecting

Detail of **Steampunk Reverie**

with the golds and bronzes in the clockface. Hooking the raven in those warm tones brings the eye down through the composition and breaks up the overwhelming cool color palette.

The clockface forms a major part of the background. It frames Charlotte and provides a focal point for the rug. Clocks and timepieces are important elements in Steampunk, and I wanted the clock to be a major part of the composition. The trim is warm gold and the clockface is a soft alternating gold and cinnamon stripe. To offset the warm colors, I used deep navy blue for the outer edge of the face, which is a lovely foil for the gold numerals. Only one clock hand is visible, pointing to the three on the right. It adds some mystery to the design; what time is it? Having two hands on the face was too cluttered.

Moving to the background, I wanted something basic and not too busy. I had decided that the lime green in the bow on top of her hat should be the same lime green in the lower portion of the rug, so that became the ivy. Ivy looks good against brick, so that settled the background for me. The brick wall is behind her and behind the clock; above the wall, you see the foggy skyline of town. The bricks are patterned after the bricks in the ranch-style house I grew up in. When I emailed a photo of the rug in progress to my sister, she immediately commented, "Those are the bricks from our house!"

Hooking bricks and mortar is not difficult, but it's important to be consistent in the texture. I put shadows on the wall to keep the wall in the background behind her. There are changes in the color values that define the shading on the bricks. Shading does not mean adding black or gray to a subject. Believable shadows have to be composed of the colors they are covering.

Once the brick wall was finished and the ledge above it was in place, I started the town. It had to be simple and soft so it stayed in the background. The town has no embellishments because they would make it come forward in the composition. The night sky above the town is a monochromatic, stylized skyline with a mysterious dirigible sailing quietly along. There are clocks in the background, but they are simply circles of light.

I left the lower section with ivy simple, but the raven seems to be looking at something, so I tucked something into that lower left-hand corner: a big blue scarab beetle with gears on his leg joints

Detail of **Steampunk Reverie**

is creeping up from behind a leaf of ivy. I hooked the carapace and realized it was shaped like an eye, so I added an eye to it. It is odd, but it's also totally in keeping with Steampunk design.

I initially drew up an elaborate carved wooden frame as the border, but it occurred to me halfway through that the frame was too traditional and needed to feel more Steampunk-y. I looked over my resources and it hit me: steam pipes! It made perfect sense. I drew in metal pipes, joints, and handles and gauges to make it real.

I like to allow a design to evolve as I work. I start with the general idea, draw the basic layout, and then take it from there. Very rarely does a rug start and finish with the original design plan intact. I move from one area to the next and modify things as I go. Each element relates to the next, and sometimes I'm inspired to change something. If they don't connect, I don't panic. I wait to see what my next inspiration is and then take it from there.

When I changed the border, I reviewed my color palette. Because I had made a dramatic change in color and texture from carved wood to smooth metal, I had to make sure the new cool colors on the outside would still work with the interior design. Because I had used cool colors like teal, gray, blue and turquoise, I wanted to make sure the added grays of the pipes would not become too repetitive.

The pipes were the last element to be hooked. I switched from a #3 cut to a #4 cut to make the pipes smoother and flatter. I chose the shading so the light came from the left, making the highlights on the left side of both vertical pipes and on the tops of the two horizontal ones. They are hooked in long, straight rows to mimic the smooth texture of metal pipe, and the joints are hooked in with the edges extending beyond the edge of the framing pipes. I hooked in a couple handles and a pressure gauge for some added color and visual interest.

Then I whipped the edge and set about attaching the collection of goodies I had gathered for the rug. I first took the navy grosgrain ribbon and made a running stitch up the middle and then gathered it to make it a ruffle; this is called ruching. I stitched the ruched ribbon into place in the unhooked areas of the bodice, where it nestled snugly against the hooked loops. In areas where the ribbon didn't cover, I went back with a hook and wool strips and filled in the blank spots.

Detail of **Steampunk Reverie**

Next I started putting the metal gears, various pieces of jewelry, and brads in place. Some had to be stitched by hand, others were tucked through the linen and opened on the back as metal brads. I had hooked a gear as a brooch on her collar and then decided to attach something else over it, so I took a metal frame and added some tiny keys and a dangle of rhinestones, then quickly made a template to fill the frame. I hooked a letter C for Charlotte and tucked it into the metal frame and mounted it on the area for a brooch.

Little metal handles found at a scrapbook store belonged around the pipes here and there. Once all the parts were secured, I took the rug outside and placed it flat on the ground so I could see it.

I was thrilled with how well it turned out. It's a rug that I was able to hook very quickly and without a lot of changes, which is unusual for me. It accomplishes everything I wanted it to, from the colors and the textures to the embellishments and style. There is a harmony and balance to the rug that pleases me.

I've enjoyed hooking all of my rugs, but this is one rug I will always cherish. It represents the culmination of everything I've learned as a rug hooker and artist, and gives me a sense of real accomplishment. Thanks, Charlotte!

CHAPTER 12

Mother Goose, or How to Revive a Lost Love

Mother Goose (See a larger view on page 105.)

Original design

MOTHER GOOSE, VERSION #1

Years ago, I started a Mother Goose rug. I have always loved nursery rhymes and fairy tales, and hooking a rug with that theme appealed to me. I was excited to begin.

I drew up a design on tracing paper with a big white goose standing in a meadow. I added nursery rhyme characters at her feet, and using colored pencils, created a color layout. It was simple and sweet and I felt like it would be a great rug.

It didn't take long to draw it up on linen in a 16″ x 22″ inch vertical format. I started hooking Mother Goose, the central figure, and I liked her face immediately. She had personality! I had drawn in Mary, Mary Quite Contrary; Humpty

Dumpty; a pumpkin to represent Peter Pumpkin Eater; and a black sheep. It was simple and basic. I was hooking in five and six cuts at that time, so I didn't try to make the characters very detailed.

But I did want the characters to have charm and personality. I found they were just too small to be

Whenever I hit a roadblock in a project, I lay everything out and ask myself what I like and what I don't like. This helps me focus on the problem areas and figure out what needs to be changed.

Hooking on my original design begins—and ends!

hooked with the detail I wanted. I decided to re-draw the design in a larger format, so I enlarged it to 26″ x 33″ . I transferred the drawing to linen . . . and then simply ignored it.

I know why I ignored it; I think I was beginning to feel that it was getting to be too much work. I liked how Mother Goose's face had turned out on the smaller rug, but I didn't think it was going to hold up in the larger rug. The design was lacking something and I just couldn't get excited about it anymore. I rolled it up and put it away.

MOTHER GOOSE, FINISHED AT LAST!

Fast forward to the present. I had completed my second Steampunk-style rug and felt the urge to go in a different direction. I like to explore new challenges and not get stuck in a design rut, so I pulled out the original drawings of Mother Goose to see what went awry. Whenever I hit a roadblock in a project, I lay everything out and ask myself what I like and what I don't like. This helps me focus on problem areas and figure out what needs to be changed.

I still wanted Mother Goose to be a central image, but the setting was uninspired and the color scheme was wishy-washy. The characters were still ill-defined and the background was, well, boring.

No wonder I walked away from it.

My hooking abilities now are greater than when I first drew up the design; now I feel more confident about using smaller cuts to get the detail I want. Instead of five and six cuts, I would use threes. I knew that creating a more interesting setting would give a better focus for the goose and the characters, so I chose an interior rather than exterior setting. After my work on Steampunk designs, I have a deep affection for and greater familiarity with Victorian styles, so I set the characters in that time and style. I choose a Victorian library with a large window as the backdrop. I collected old photos found online of Victorian clothing and children in various settings that would lend themselves to the nursery rhymes.

I discovered that the Victorians were the original "Photoshoppers." They explored the new magic of photography with many different techniques. There are quite a few examples of Victorian photographs of people with animal heads, which some people find disconcerting, but I enjoy. I immediately decided to make my Mother Goose as a woman with a goose neck and head. I found a photo of a young woman in profile, wearing a voluminous satin gown and sitting in a chair, reading a book. She was perfect!

Detail of **Mother Goose** (See the full rug on page 105.)

Once I had established the goose figure, it was time to choose the nursery rhyme characters. I found a photo of a boy tying his shoes, which became buckled shoes. A boy on a hobby horse became Ride a Cock Horse to Banbury Cross. A solemn-faced young girl standing by a staircase became Mary Quite Contrary. Peter Pumpkin and his wife were assigned to a big round pumpkin, and Humpty Dumpty was a figure of my own imagination.

There was a cow jumping over the moon in the original design, and I still liked the idea of having something of interest in the background, so I drew in a cow and moon on the right-hand side of the design. I focused the central area of the rug with a window frame, giving a sense of place for the room and a foil for the main characters. And I designed a landscape with a wide-open sky with clouds for the background scene.

I wanted this rug to be rich with color and pattern and images. I had learned from *Steampunk*

Reverie that using a limited color palette was extremely helpful in executing the overall design. With so many elements, using unlimited colors would make the rug too jumbled and disjointed. So I selected a few main colors and used that limited palette to create a cohesive and coordinated design. I chose the secondary color palette combination of orange, green, and purple.

I haven't used the color orange very often in my rug hooking career, and with Mother Goose's beak and the pumpkin, I decided to make that a key color. I wanted a rich warm green that would go nicely with the orange, and then decided that purple would be the third major color, and the choice for the wonderful gown. The gown is definitely a key element in the big picture, and it takes up a lot of area, as does her bonnet, which is also purple. Other smaller bits of the rug have purple, but not a lot. I did play a joke by making the cow purple and brown, based on the Gelett Burgess poem about a purple cow:

With so many elements, using unlimited colors would make the rug too jumbled and disjointed. So I selected a few main colors and used that limited palette to create a cohesive and coordinated design.

Detail of **Mother Goose** (See the full rug on page 105.)

I never saw a purple cow,
I never hope to see one,
But I can tell you, anyhow,
I'd rather see than be one.

When you use a limited palette, it's important to assign colors all across the rug so they are evenly distributed and they create a movement on the surface that seems natural and fluid. In this case, even though there are many elements in orange, they are all slightly different. The beak is a fairly bright shade with several values of orange in it. The pumpkin is rich and vibrant, too, but not as brightly contrasted as the beak. The boy on the horse is wearing an orange jacket, but it's darker and duller, and Mary Quite Contrary is a "ginger," a redhead, using those oranges.

The green is a major player in the wallpaper, but it's dark and subtle. It plays a supporting role across the rug: as a sash for the purple gown, in Mary's dress, Peter's shirt, Buckle Boy's pants, and also the pants and tie for the horse-riding boy. It makes a strong cool color against the orange and provides a solid companion for the purple.

The bright blues are in smaller quantities: another cool color that appears in Mother Goose's eye, Humpty's suit, in Peter's wife's dress, and the saddle of the horse. There is also blue shading in the feathers of Mother Goose's shoulder. It's a minor role, but a nice touch in the color scheme.

The sky also needed to fit the color scheme. In college, I had painted a glowing sunset landscape with a big cloud in the sky, and the colors of that painting—warm oranges, peaches, and purples— were perfect for the rug. We tend to think of blue skies, but sometimes skies are anything but blue. Having the sky in those twilight colors made sense, especially since the moon is out for the cow to jump over. It fit the color palette and it gave a sense of continuity.

But that's when things got weird.

Mother Goose underway

I tried four times to hook a cloudy twilight sky. I tried using my cloud painting as a source. I tried using a good color photo as a guide. I used colors that I had already used in the rug. I changed the direction of the clouds and hooked from the horizon up halfway. And it was all wrong.

I finally realized that I had already subconsciously planned the color of the sky when I hooked the moon and purple cow. It was not twilight or dawn, it was nighttime. Mother Goose was never going to show up against a lighter-colored sky, nor would she be the central focus against a sky filled with clouds. I wanted the moon to glow and the cow to show up clearly, and that wasn't going to work against medium values.

Ripping out the sky for the third time, I began to wonder if there were any options left if the dark sky didn't work. But I had dyed more deep navy blue and a couple of other purple and blue combinations and I was going ahead.

Instead of hooking the area of sky in the lower left, as I had done previously, I started hooking around the cow and moon with the dark navy blue.

The sky, first idea

Detail of checkerboard frame

As that area of sky filled and the moon really started to glow, I knew I had finally gotten it right. I did incorporate some dim purple clouds along the horizon line for some break in the solid blue, and the sky finally started making sense.

Since I had left the upper left area of background plain, the navy color was going to need something to break it up. What can be in a night sky? Stars! I quickly thought about constellations and looked up the star pattern for my zodiac sign, which is Pisces. The constellation has a nice diagonal flow to it and would be perfect for that space. So I drew in the stars and hooked each one with a white loop. Then it was just all about filling in the rest of the sky.

And isn't it perfect that she's reading bedtime nursery rhymes?

With the night sky, the background was complete. My next challenge was the border. I had planned to use alternating squares to represent the black and white checkered edge from the cover of my old Rand McNally *The Real Mother Goose* by Blanche Fisher Wright. But rather than use black and white, I used a dark navy blue and a cream to keep the colors within the palette I had chosen. At first glance, it may seem to be black and white, but the deep blue and cream are more compatible with the rug's scheme.

Now for finishing. I chose a dyed wool yarn to whip the edges. It's a cinnamon color, which is the same color I used in the window frame and in other areas of the rug. By using this color, I made a connection between the inside of the rug and the edge, which helps to move the eye around the rug.

I learned a lot from this rug. I learned more about myself and my ability to persevere than I ever have before in creating a rug. I learned that just because something doesn't work, you don't have to give up.

Rx FOR A TROUBLESOME RUG

So how do you keep yourself from just giving up? Whether you have purchased a pattern designed by someone else or designed it yourself, when you hit a wall, ask yourself why. Why now? At some point, you fell in love with the design and then something happened. In my case with *Mother Goose,* I was not limited by my vision or imagination, but by my lack of experience at the time. I knew I wouldn't be able to render that image the way I wanted to, and so I set it aside.

But sometimes the difficulties can be faced and fixed. Lay the rug out in the clear light of day and take a hard look at it. Make a list. What are the good points? Do you like the color palette? Is there a good balance of color, light and dark, bright and dull? Are the elements in the rug well defined? How about depth and perspective? Do some elements come forward and others recede? Is there a motion in the design that leads the eye around the rug?

Figuring out what is holding you back isn't always easy, but with some careful evaluation the problems can usually be identified. If you are completely stumped, ask someone else for an opinion. Often we cannot determine what the problem is because we can't see it objectively. A fresh pair of eyes might help figure out what went awry.

Sometimes we set a rug aside because it's not a challenge anymore and we are bored. Let's face it: there are rugs that seemed like a great idea at the time and just died on the vine. But if you've invested time and wool in a dud, take another look just in case it can be revived. Sometimes it's as simple as adding a few more colors, or changing the focus of the design. Maybe it's a matter of reworking small segments to brighten part of the rug, or parts that need to be darkened for contrast. The play between light and dark is a valuable tool in design, and a monotonous color scheme can be simply too dull or boring. Maybe add some outlines around key elements, or cast shadows or re-define certain areas of the rug to see if the definition will change and bring the rug back to life. Sometimes a small fix applied to certain parts of a rug will yield great results, getting you focused and excited again. It's like reviving a lost love.

Chapter 13

Conclusion

I've been an artist all my life. I have explored different means of self-expression—drawing, painting, sculpture—and I have found rug hooking to be the perfect way for me to do what I seem to have been born to do: make art.

Everything about rug hooking is what art is for me. It contains all of the elements: line, color, composition, contrast, scale, and design. The wonderful element for me is texture, which makes the art form a touchable, tactile pleasure. It's warm and dense, unlike the cold flat surface of paintings. It's the best of everything in my creative wheelhouse.

We are artists. Rug hookers create art with value. We create history, we document life, we make heirlooms. Rug hookers are a creative force who need to recognize the value of what we do.

We need to share our work, teach our art, give of ourselves so that our art stays viable and alive.

I hope this book will give you—rug hooking artists yourselves—some insights, inspiration, and ideas about rug hooking. I hope there are techniques here that will solve problems, provide information, and spark a creative urge that makes rug hookers want to start a new project or shake some life into a stale one.

There are a million rugs out there, waiting to be made. We had all better get busy!

CHAPTER 14

Gallery of Rugs

Koi, 30" x 30", #5-, 6- and 8-cut wool on linen.
Designed and hooked by Donna Hrkman, Dayton, Ohio, 2004.

Native American Boy, 28" x 33", #3-cut wool on linen.
Designed and hooked by Donna Hrkman, Dayton, Ohio, 2011.

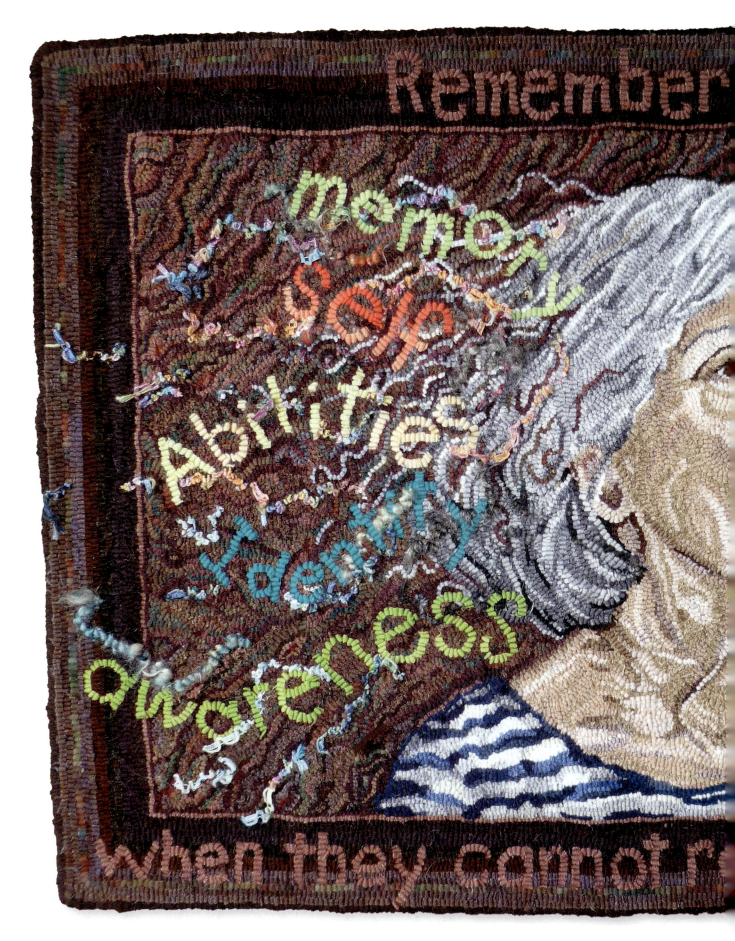

Alzheimer's Rug,
23" x 29", #3- and
5-cut wool on linen.
Designed and hooked
by Donna Hrkman,
Dayton, Ohio, 2012.

Red-Eared Turtle, 30" x 24", #6-cut wool on linen.
Designed and hooked by Donna Hrkman, Dayton, Ohio, 2008.

Veteran's Day, 29" x 35", #3-, 4-, 5-, and 6-cut wool on linen.
Designed and hooked by Donna Hrkman, Dayton, Ohio, 2010.

Blue Mermaiden,
18" x 26", #3-cut
wool on linen.
Designed and
hooked by Donna
Hrkman, Dayton,
Ohio, 2013.

Three French Hens, 16" x 12", #8-cut wool on linen. Designed and hooked by Donna Hrkman, Dayton, Ohio, 2005.

Pink Flamingo Cottage, 19" x 34", #3-, 5-, and 6-cut wool on linen.
Designed and hooked by Donna Hrkman, Dayton, Ohio, 2009.

Steampunk Polly, 18" x 25½", #3-cut wool on linen.
Designed and hooked by Donna Hrkman, Dayton, Ohio, 2014.

Steampunk Reverie, 33" x 43", #3-, 4-, and 5-cut wool on linen.
Designed and hooked by Donna Hrkman, Dayton, Ohio, 2014.

Sunflower Girl, 26" x 18", #3-, 4-, and 5-cut wool on linen. Designed and hooked by Donna Hrkman, Dayton, Ohio, 2012.

Barred Owl, 26" x 30", #4-, 6-, and 8-cut wool on linen.
Designed and hooked by Donna Hrkman, Dayton, Ohio, 2006.

Mother Goose, 36" x 46", #3-cut wool on linen.
Designed and hooked by Donna Hrkman, Dayton, Ohio, 2015.